The Let's Series of ESL

INSTRUCTOR'S
HANDBOOK

The Let's Series of ESL

The Let's Series of ESL
INSTRUCTOR'S HANDBOOK

William Samelson

ELSTREET
EDUCATIONAL
Baltimore • Washington

ISBN: 978-0-935437-35-5

EDUCATIONAL
PO Box 858
Savage
800-296-1961
www.Elstreet.com

Cover Illustrations by Edward Molina
Cover Design by Ross Feldner

Printed in the United States of America

Contents

INTRODUCTION

Rationale For the Development of Five Separate Texts

L anguage instruction has undergone reevaluation and many changes in the past decade. For many years students of languages have been overwhelmed by an overabundance of learning matter within one given period of time, while a single text was used to fulfill the task of explaining the four skills; listening-speaking, reading comprehension, and writing. The same is true of the teacher who finds it difficult to try and keep these skills apart in order to facilitate learning.

Some instructors may feel that the development of the oral skills (listening-speaking) are more desirable for their teaching situation. Others may find it necessary to stress the importance of reading, or others still might desire to emphasize the skill of writing and rhetoric for their purposes and the special needs of their students. All teachers agree that each skill is equally important in new language acquisition.

During the development of the present project of teaching basic English, we have recognized yet another necessity inherent in teaching. We prepared the ESL texts each dealing with a distinct aspect of language learning as the titles indicate. This was motivated by the following question: "What if a student has the need for and desires only to learn to converse in the language? Why should this individual be subjected to the same timetable as the student desiring to study writing or reading?" It was clear to see that in many instances time was being wasted following an outline of a text not limited to the particular skill desired.

We have decided to offer the learner a choice whereby he/she can study one skill at a time. This greatly simplifies the student's task of concentrating on the desired goal; it also makes teaching less complicated and more precise. Thus, the initial text, *Phase Zero Plus: Let's Begin,* introduces students to the essentials of English; we dedicate three texts, *Phase One* through *Phase Three,* to learning one skill at a time. Following that, we round up our study with *Phase Four* which once again goes deeply into the four skills: listening, speaking, reading and writing.

This approach to learning one skill at a time is of great importance to our ESL series. Each of the texts contains original dialogues and stories pertaining to everyday life in the U.S.. They appear in common, everyday vocabulary (so often neglected in introductory language courses), stressing primarily those events which will give the learner a mastery in the fundamentals of the language as well as a good grasp of situations in the U.S. ranging from campus life to a doctor's office, a shopping trip, in a restaurant, in the city, getting a job, banking, etc. Most importantly, we are dealing here with a functional everyday American English which gives the student an opportunity to manipulate and personalize the language. Moreover, all conversations and model compositions are short and easily learned. In addition, they each include only previously learned vocabulary and grammatical points so that the students are not confused by arbitrary introduction of new forms which they cannot recognize.

Significance of Phases

Proceeding through the five Phases of the *LET'S SERIES* from *Phase Zero-Plus: Let's Begin* to *Phase Four: Let's Continue,* the series is based on the premise that students who have little or no knowledge of English at the beginning of their study are expected to achieve the level of near native English proficiency. The texts, as well as the testing methods, are *designed* with the above goal in mind. The Phases indicate proficiency levels. We can safely assume that, if the criterion for total proficiency characterized by the number 5 in a given language is that of an educated native, and a complete ignorance of the language is characterized by the numerical designator 0, the highest goal of achievement upon completion of this text series is expected to reach the proficiency level three (3). The level of language proficiency reflects the productive competence of students in a given language. For reasons of clarifying the design of the *LET'S SERIES,* as well as the criterion-referenced evaluation of language competency, we have provided below a step by step outline of text material to be covered in order that a certain level of language proficiency might be reached.

0 to 1— From no knowledge at all to survivorship (able to satisfy routine travel needs and minimum courtesy requirements).

Phase Zero-Plus: Let's Begin

1+ to 2 — From survivorship to working proficiency (able to satisfy routine social demands and limited work requirements. Can read and write simple authentic material on subjects within a familiar context).

Phase One: Let's Converse
Phase Two: Let's Read
Phase Three: Let's Write

2+ to 3 — From working proficiency to minimum proficiency. (able to speak the language with sufficient structural accuracy and vocabulary to participate effectively in most formal and informal conversations on practical, social, and professional topics). Able to read standard newspaper items addressed to the general reader, routine correspondence, reports and technical material in own special field.

Phase Four: Let's Continue

Appendices as an Aid to Learning

To aid students with retention of the material covered, each book of the ESL LET'S SERIES includes an "Appendix." Basically a summary or overview of key elements learned, the following are sections in the order of their appearance:

Let's Begin
Active Vocabulary
Some Irregular Verbs
Some Regular Adjectives and Adverbs
Some Irregular Comparative Forms of Some Adjectives and
    Adverbs
Index

Let's Converse
Active Vocabulary
Instructions to the Applicant
Applications to file petition for naturalization
Index

Let's Read
Active Vocabulary
Index

Let's Write
Active Vocabulary
Principal Parts of Irregular Verbs
Parts of Speech
Index

Let's Continue
Active Vocabulary
Two-Word Verbs
Compound Prepositions
Transitional Words and Phrases
Index

Supplements

In addition to the student texts and the *Instructors Handbook,* CD's and/or cassettes are available for each of the chapters in *Let's Begin, Let's Converse,* and *Let's Continue.* These are recordings of all oral-aural practice material, including dramatizations of the dialogues found in each of the texts mentioned. In all, we have three hours of listening time. This is distributed in the following way:

Let's Begin = CD or Cassette, 53 minutes of listening time.

Let's Converse = CD or Cassette, 58 minutes of listening time.

Let's Continue = CD or Cassette, 60 minutes of listening time.

Each recorded lesson touches on the highlights of the Chapter, such as dialogues, pronunciation drills and audio-lingual exercises. The length of each chapter's recording varies from 5 to 8 minutes of dramatization. Pauses for student repetition and imitation are inserted, and the recordings can be used in a laboratory, classroom situation, or private surroundings.

A slowly executed drill can become monotonous. Too much choral or individual repetition can result in boredom. For this reason the repetition drills are short. Voices are those of native speakers from various parts of the United States representing a cross-section of "standard" American English pronunciation. There are male and female voices. The melodies of folk songs to be learned in *Let's Begin* and *Let's Continue* are rendered on the piano. These can be used as accompaniment for classroom singing sessions.

Evaluations

Our *Instructor's Handbook* contains a series of evaluations. They begin with placement, continue with analyzing progress, and culminate with achievement evaluations. All evaluations can be administered to groups of students or individually. They can be scored easily in very little time.

Procedures for student ESL Certification complete the evaluative process. Techniques in evaluating linguistic competence as well as the recording of such findings are thoroughly outlined, making this an innovative and invaluable guide for the ESL teacher.

Summary

The successful completion of the entire *LET'S SERIES* carries with it a specific promise for the individual ESL student. In fact, we may predict with a reasonable degree of assurance that the student shall achieve the level of linguistic effectiveness measured in the TOEFL Examination by a scale of 500. This goal in itself, if achieved, will open the doors of most United States universities and colleges to the foreign student desiring to enter them.

As has been stated, the design of the *LET'S SERIES* of ESL texts is such that its objectives and goals meet the criteria of specific "steps" of instruction. Briefly reviewed, this means that, for example, students who begin their course of study at the zero level of competence (Text *Zero Plus: Let's Begin*) will generally reach the level of "one" at the completion of this text. Each student's proficiency is evaluated according to his/her own achievement rather than by peer comparison. It further follows that, provided all steps of study are thoroughly pursued, students are expected to reach the highest level of speaking, reading, and writing proficiency in their language study when they have completed *Phase Four: Let's Continue*. Considered on a universal scale of rating, the *Phase Four* student is expected to reach the S-3 (see Check-list to Determine Ratings, p. 257) level of competence provided all learning processes have been exploited in great detail. The expected proficiency for a student with a given background and a given aptitude, after a given number of semesters, will depend not only on the difficulty of the language itself, but also on the amount of time and effort expended by the student in concurrent study—as well as on the individual's desire and motivation to learn and achieve his/her goals.

THE STRUCTURE OF THE TEXTS

The "General Remarks" as well as the section following it, "Teaching Suggestions," are offered here at the urging of classroom teachers who have used and experimented with the "Let's" texts prior to their final, present format. These suggestions may or may not be suitable for every classroom situation. In every teaching environment, it is the teacher who must determine the student's needs. Thus, the teacher must select or reject a particular methodology in order to best fulfill the demands of a particular learning situation. The remarks that follow, however, are intended to maximize the teaching and learning potential under most circumstances.

Each chapter of the five texts is broken down into ten (10) important sections:

The Dialogues in each of the five texts as well as the Narratives (Model Compositions), contain only those structural or grammatical items which the students are to learn in a given chapter. In this manner, the students are able to comprehend the material without having to analyze structural forms as yet unlearned. Also grammatical structures are learned inductively and naturally. Rote memorization is avoided at all cost and boredom or lack of interest are prevented. Any vocabulary items used initially are repeated in subsequent chapters. This repetition in different context gives students an opportunity to thoroughly familiarize themselves with each new word under a variety of circumstances. It makes words more meaningful and their application manifold and rich. All of the words are listed in the Active Vocabulary sections in the Appendices with annotations indicating the chapter in which the word was used for the first time.

Oftentimes, however, stylistically preferable forms have been avoided in favor of simpler forms within the grasp of the students at their particular stage of language development. As the students progress through the text series and develop a greater command of the language, the level of selection becomes more sophisticated.

Now, a few remarks about each of the texts:

LET'S BEGIN

Phase Zero Plus: Let's Begin is the first step in learning English as a second language. *Let's Begin* is designed either for classroom use or for individual study with or without an instructor. The book is intended for students on the elementary level of their study of English, regardless of age.

Line drawings are plentiful, offering the students an outlet for the repeated use of newly learned vocabulary in describing the great variety of situations. Emphasis is in repetition not memorization. It is by using words in context that the students are gradually able to find their way to free expression and free writing. Learning is cumulative, based on a solid foundation.

The text does not presuppose any previous knowledge of basic grammar and verb usage. All chapters allow for the teaching of certain basic forms of grammar and syntax. There is a minimum of formal explanation. Instead, new items of grammar are introduced in each chapter by pattern practice and constantly reinforced in succeeding lessons.

Let's Begin is aimed at students who are natives of foreign countries wishing to acquire a basic level of English proficiency in an English-speaking environment.

Hence, the primary objective of *Let's Begin* is to afford the student a fair comprehension of the language as well as the ability of active expression in American English, both spoken and written. The text undertakes to present learning situations other than those usually encountered in the classroom. For that purpose, a variety of up-to-date short readings and dialogues have been composed. They allow students easy access to everyday vocabulary and freedom to use the words in their own limited self-expression. Vocabulary is repeated and augmented with each additional chapter. This method provides a facility for memorization through repetition.

It is hoped that *Let's Begin* will enable students of English as a Second Language to enjoy their study experience. Our concern here is to provide a challenging text so that both teacher and student alike may become involved in a productive and rewarding activity of guiding and learning respectively. The end result of such activity will, hopefully, yield communicative confidence in all four skills; listening, speaking, reading, and writing on a basic level.

A word about the format is in order.

An attempt is made to present all lessons in a uniform manner, leading to appropriate exercises and pattern drills throughout the text. This is done to reinforce the learned material.

There is a noticeable gradation in the presentation of all new learning material, varying in degree of sophistication while keeping step with the student's progressive acquisition of knowledge and communicative confidence. This process increases the incentive for learning while it eliminates boredom and the element of guesswork.

Each chapter is divided into sections. The heading of the section indicates in simple terms what the student is to do: READ, LISTEN/ TALK, COPY, PRONUNCIATION PRACTICE, IDENTIFY, COM- PLETE, GUESS WHO?, GIVE THE NAME, etc.

Each section fulfills a specific function within the chapter. Therefore, an attempt should be made to complete them all. However, the order and extent of coverage of the individual sections is left up to the discretion of the instructor. The section approach makes it possible for the instructor to determine the order of presentation of material best suited for the needs of the students. Each section is constructed in a manner that lends itself for the presentation of the grammatical items which are to be learned within the given chapter. Each section is properly graded not to represent material beyond that already studied.

In deference to those students not familiar with the Roman alphabet, a "Preliminary Chapter" briefly touching on penmanship is included. This is an added feature and serves as a "warm-up" for the COPY or LISTEN and WRITE exercises to follow in subsequent chapters. Also discussed in this chapter are matters concerning spelling and syllabification. These are all supplementary items and can be omitted when and if a classroom situation warrants their omission.

Among other attractive and useful features of *Let's Begin* are the UNSCRAMBLE THE LETTERS exercises and the WORD PUZZLES. These types of exercises serve to emphasize spelling awareness and make it interesting for students to increase their word power.

A familiar American PROVERB, illustrated to facilitate comprehension, completes each chapter to further the student's appreciation of life and customs in the United States of America.

The introductory section READ describes a SITUATION which will help the student to understand the grammar principles introduced in the chapter. The SITUATION will also serve in preparing students to personalize and recreate at a later time the dialogue which follows it.

The LISTEN/TALK section is used as a follow-up to the SITUATION. It provides students with the opportunity to practice the lines of the dialogue aloud, as in role-playing. It further stimulates them to actively amplify their communicative skill, depending on the degree of creative ability and the extent of their progress.

The LISTEN/TALK section can be memorized if needed, because it is short and conversational in form. It deals with interesting topics relating to everyday life. It is essential that students master both READ and LISTEN/TALK sections before continuing with the material that follows. READ and LISTEN/TALK are the core sections of each chapter.

In addition to the LISTEN/TALK section, there are EXTRA DIALOGUES featured in many chapters. These serve to illustrate some point of grammar or emphasize newly-learned vocabulary in a practical setting. These short encounters can also be memorized and acted out by students in a classroom. This feature gives the learner an opportunity to personalize the context of the lesson for greater depth of comprehension and ultimate retention of material learned.

The COPY section serves as writing practice, especially for those students whose language does not utilize the Roman alphabet as its model for writing. The initial chapters provide patterns to COPY, both in printed and cursive form. Later on in the text, as the student becomes accustomed to using the Roman alphabet, the cursive part is left out. Beginning with chapter 4, some COPY exercises are converted into LISTEN and WRITE (Dictation) practice.

The aim of *Let's Begin* is to enable non-English speaking students to understand speakers of English and to communicate their basic needs to them. To this end, the exercises and practice sections are presented, which provide learning experiences in listening, talking, reading and writing. The exercises are varied and their scope geared toward grammar-based activities. In the more advanced texts of this series, Phases I, II, III and IV, emphasis is placed on contextualization and function-based exercises.

The listening materials are indicated throughout the text with a drawing of a student wearing a headset and listening in a language lab. These drills afford the student additional voice intonation other than that of the classroom instructor. Written exercises test and reinforce student comprehension and progress.

The initial SITUATIONS and DIALOGUES are developed to teach a variety of topics. These include survival skills, such as asking questions about things and people, riding a bus, ordering food in a restaurant, and dealing with questions of time and money. The talking materials are designed to help students role-play, using American English in a variety of interactional situations.

The overall goal of *Let's Begin* is to help develop the essential skills of "Zero Plus" knowledge which are a must if the student is to continue on the way to communicative competence in further studies of English. Those basic aspects of the language acquired here are: a cultural appreciation, reading comprehension, writing ability, vocabulary building and conversation. I am hopeful that the interesting and timely topics presented here will help make the study of American English a pleasurable experience, and one that will encourage the student to further exploration of our rich language.

LET'S CONVERSE

Phase One: Let's Converse is intended as a beginning text in conversational English. The book is designed for a one semester course. One of the main advantages of this text is that its scope is limited. It is a language course with complete focus on speaking.

Let's Converse is primarily aimed at an adult college student, whether native English-speaking with the need for remedial learning, or a native of a foreign country wishing to live or study in an English-speaking environment. However, utilizing its context appropriately, the book may also be found useful for the instruction of students of high school age.

A few words about the format of the book are in order.

Let's Converse is composed of ten chapters. Each chapter is divided into ten sections. Each of the sections fulfills a specific function within the chapter. An attempt should, therefore, be made to complete them all. However, the order and extent of coverage of these sections is left up to the discretion of the instructor. The section approach makes it possible for the instructor to determine the order of presentation of material best suited for the needs of a class.

ORAL EXERCISE

Each *Oral Exercise* deals with everyday situations and contains everyday words and phrases. Each dialogue is a sequence of normal speech responses to a given situation. The teacher goes through the dialogue with the students repeating and imitating the sounds. Questions should be asked to see if the students understand the meaning. Its contextual presentation is such that the words and grammatical structures become obvious in meaning. The student learns to handle whole dialogues from the very outset. Repeated association and use of words make memorization of sentence patterns unnecessary. The structure present in the dialogue will recur in the following nine sections. The student is thus reinforced in what is learned in the dialogue.

WORDS and QUESTIONS

The vocabulary found in the dialogue is presented alphabetically. The teacher reads aloud. Students repeat with books closed. Letters in **bold print** should be pronounced louder to produce the proper prounciation. Students must become familiar with these words and repeat them in context. By the time the students have reached the exercises of each chapter, these words should be part of their active vocabulary.

PRONUNCIATION DRILL

For each section (except 10) a few typical sounds have been selected for a short drill. Altogether, when we have reached Chapter 9, we will have drilled most of the consonants, vowels, and diphthongs of American English. To reinforce what the students have learned during laboratory sessions, the teacher should conduct frequent evaluations of progress by giving short oral quizzes in class.

PHRASES (STRUCTURES)

These incomplete *phrases* should be written on the chalkboard. Students are to convert the fragments into complete sentences. These phrases are presented in the sequence in which they occur in the dialogue. Students are asked to pronounce each phrase aloud as it is written on the board. Use of transparencies is desired.

SENTENCES

The isolated are now complete, but simple, sentences. They further emphasize patterns used in talking. They present frequent morphological items and most structure words.

STATEMENTS

Students are now given the briefest of dialogue situations which are taken out of context. This affords them a better look at the flexibility of the language they have mastered so far. It widens the students' language perspective and the scope of their articulation.

VOCABULARY BUILDING

Students are now presented with words (taken from the dialogue) in a range of their major semantic environments. This will prevent the students from developing a fixed association between one word-one meaning.

GRAMMAR

In this section we attempt to satisfy the analytical mind of the student. There are complete paradigmatic sets, where necessary, in reference to previously learned items. Grammatical comments are offered within the framework of each dialogue. These should be augmented by the teacher whenever the need arises. The teacher may find it unnecessary to cover this entire section during the class period. Rather, the student who feels that it will help him/her to know the mechanics of a foreign language may be encouraged to absorb these grammatical explanations through private study.

PRACTICE

After the students have learned the dialogue, various occurrences of structural nature are isolated as patterns. These pattern-drills help in forming speech habits. The teacher will explain that the pattern is a frame which can be used in various situations. The only change involved is that of vocabulary. Students may be encouraged to compose new dialogue using similar structural pattern but changing the situation.

The practice patterns are of such nature that it becomes possible for the students to develop a fluency in the language without an especial stress on grammar. The teacher should not feel compelled to use all of the practice drills in the text. Some are more difficult and should be attempted only in exceptional classes. Others can be used for testing purposes. The abundance of drills and exercises gives the instructor more latitude in the use of this text.

EXERCISES

The combined exercises bring together the grammar points learned in this chapter for intensive work and review.

The abundance of exercises is only intended as a convenience to be used at the discretion of the teacher. It should become an enjoyable experience for both student and teacher rather than an arbitrary work-load.

IDIOMS

A portion of the text presents selected words as they are used idiomatically. Idioms become particularly important to foreign speakers when they realize that many idioms have an equivalent in their native tongues. However, the teacher should explain that a literal rendition of an idiom into another language would, for the most part, prove inaccurate, if not embarrassing. Idioms are presented as brief sections. Some chapters are also adorned with an appropriate saying or poem, and we should encourage students to learn the content.

Finally, the author believes that one of the most exciting features of this text is that it gives the student time to achieve success. No one in the classroom must feel that he/she has to push in order to complete the text. Because of the abundance of material, we may all feel free to stop on occasions, to review, to reemphasize, and to spot-test.

Flexibility is essential in making the learning process a successful enterprise.

LET'S READ

Phase Two: Let's Read is to be used as an introductory reader for students of English as a Second Language. The book is intended for a one-semester intensive course. We assume that the student has a basic knowledge of spoken English. This text aims at enlarging the student's passive (cognitive) vocabulary for better comprehension of written material. Hopefully, with intensive practice, passive comprehension will be converted into actively generated structures and ideas. This text reinforces structures already learned and introduces the student to different types of discourse: narrative, expository, and descriptive.

Our aim is, therefore, to provide the student with the ability to read independently and competently. To achieve the above objectives we undertake the following:

1. To combine *sight* and *sound*. Reading will be performed silently and verbally. Teacher will read aloud at first while students follow text from open books.

2. To identify word *meaning in context* rather than in *isolation*. Teacher will discuss *meaning of words in context* and answer questions *concerning structure*.

3. To heighten the student's ability to *identify* the *meaning of complete phrases* mechanically through rapid recognition. Teacher will read from the text with students' books closed. Students will discuss contents of narrative at will.

Let's Read is primarily aimed at the adult college student, whether native English-speaking with the need for *remedial learning,* or a native of a foreign country wishing to live or study in an English-speaking environment. However, by utilizing the context appropriately, the book may also be found useful for the instruction of students of high school age.

One of the main advantages of this text is that its scope is limited. It is a basic language course with emphasis on *reading*. A sincere effort has been made here to simplify without oversimplification. In this endeavor, we have been guided by our desire to make language learning easier than it is customarily experienced.

A few words about the format of the book are in order. *Let's Read* is composed of ten chapters. These chapters should be taken up in sequence for maximum effectiveness. Each chapter is divided into ten sections, and each of the sections fulfills a specific function within the chapter. An attempt should, therefore, be made to complete each of the sections. However, the order and extent of coverage of these sections are left up to the discretion of the teacher. The section approach makes it possible for the teacher to determine the order of presentation of material best suited for the needs of his/her class.

NARRATIVE

Each narrative is an original composition dealing with everyday situations and containing everyday words and phrases. All narratives are arranged according to context, whether *concrete* or *abstract*. They range from stories of general interest to those of specific interest. These narratives are for the most part simple in form, with some degree of sophistication in later chapters. Finally, there exists a length variant.

The contextual presentation of the narratives is such that grammatical and syntactical structures become obvious. The structures presented in the initial narrative will recur in the following nine. What is learned is thus reinforced, eliminating the necessity of rote memorization.

WORDS IN CONTEXT (Pictographs)

The narrative is presented in a series of *pictographs*. Words used in the narrative are listed below each pictograph. Where possible, *synonyms* and *antonyms* are printed after each word.

In this manner, the student learns new words and expressions in their varied usage within the context of a narrative. Students reconstruct the narrative using related words, in class under teacher supervision or at home. This practice will improve the learner's reading speed and comprehension. It will also offer students a wider range of vocabulary.

STRUCTURES (Phrases)

The incomplete *phrases* are the smallest, disrupted fragments of the narrative. They are to be converted orally into complete sentences. The phrases are presented in the sequence in which they occur in the narrative.

SENTENCES

The isolated *phrases* from section III have now become complete, but simple, *sentences*. The sentences are also presented in the sequence in which they occur in the narrative. They are to be read aloud. Substitution of related words for the *italicized* ones will make this exercise meaningful and not a mere rote performance.

GRAMMAR AND SYNTAX

In this section we attempt to satisfy the analytical mind of the student. There are complete paradigmatic sets where necessary in reference to the items learned. Grammatical structures offered here are presented within the framework of each narrative and should be orally identified. The teacher will find it helpful to devote a good portion of time to this section, for it will help the student to know the mechanics of the language in order to facilitate comprehension.

WORD RECOGNITION

Words are selected from the narrative. The student is given the opportunity to identify the synonym (later the antonym) of each selection. This will contribute further to building an active vocabulary. This section is to be used as a timed *diagnostic word test* in which the student defines each word studied in the narrative. New sentences may be constructed using the newly identified word.

CONCEPT RECOGNITION

Concepts contained in the narrative are chronologically listed. They are to be studied with constant reference to word recognition. This chronological study serves to reinforce recognition of concept relations and to help master grammatical order.

TELLING THE MEANING

This exercise is to be read orally. Complete sentences are to be constructed using words related in meaning to those given. This section should also be used as a timed *diagnostic word test.*

COMPREHENSION (Exercises)

A variety of comprehensive exercises is presented, testing for word-recognition, idea-patterns, and the meaning of isolated material taken from the narrative. These may be used at the discretion of the instructor. The exercises serve a double purpose: (1) their abundance gives the instructor more latitude in the use of this text; (2) they enable the student to analyze the narrative independently. These exercises should be an enjoyable experience for both the student and teacher rather than an arbitrary work load.

DISCUSSION AND EVALUATION

This section of each chapter serves as a summary for both teacher and student. Having studied the preceding sections thoroughly, the student should now be ready to read and interpret the entire narrative. He/She should undertake to discuss the story in context and, if possible, relate other experiences of similar nature.

The *evaluation* part of this section is for review and evaluation of things learned; it is presented in the form of short quizzes.

Poetry is an integral part of a language and should be introduced early in the student's language-learning process. Poems are used here as a device for improving reading comprehension and for providing an outlet for simple literary analysis. Teacher should encourage students to read the poetry selections and discuss their meaning in class.

LET'S WRITE

Phase Three: Let's Write is to be used as a text for a basic course in writing and composition for students of English as a Second Language. It is a pre-college text of English composition. The book is intended for a one-semester course though it can be used for intensive study courses also. The book aims at developing the student's vocabulary for better comprehension. It has been designed to offer the maximum limits of writing for the basic course.

It is a well-known fact that one does not write as one speaks, though both speaking and writing are communication. Thus far, the student may have learned two types of vocabulary: 1. a *speaking* vocabulary (the most limited of the vocabularies), consisting of words used in conversation; 2. a *reading* vocabulary (larger than either the *speaking* or *writing* vocabularies), containing words that can be understood on sight even though one may not be able to use them in speech or writing. *Let's Write* offers the student a third type of vocabulary: the *writing* vocabulary. This vocabulary is more extensive than that used in conversation. The present text reinforces structures learned through oral and reading comprehension while it introduces the student to the skill of writing.

Writing will be defined here as "the ability to use the language and its graphic representations in ordinary writing situations. More specifically, writing a foreign language (is) the ability to use the structures, the lexical items, and their conventional representations, in ordinary matter-of-fact writing."*

Our aim is to provide the student with the ability to write independently and competently. To achieve the above objectives we undertake the following:

1. To provide models of various types of composition (from simple one-paragraph types to a lengthy but uncomplicated term paper), which the student will copy and ultimately learn to write independently.

2. To comment briefly on each *Model Composition* and to discuss distinguishing characteristics of style and organization. This will aid the students in their own writing and increase their comprehension of written material.

3. To suggest writing topics of broad and varying difficulty. This will allow the individual student to develop a writing skill reflecting his/her unique personality, background, and attitude.

4. To further enlarge the student's active vocabulary by providing alternate meanings for selected phrases and words. These are defined in the sense of the context of the *Model Composition*. Such contextual presentation reinforces the learning process, increasing the rate of retention and motivation.

To achieve the above objectives, each chapter (except CHAPTER ONE, *THE WORD*) comprises ten sections. Each section fulfills a unique *function within* the overall aim of this text.

---

* Robert Lado, *Language Testing*, McGraw-Hill, 1964, pp. 248-9.

MODEL COMPOSITION

The initial part of the chapter serves as an example of correct writing. Students will be expected to read the *Model Composition* with total comprehension if they are to write with reasonable skill at some future time. To achieve this goal, students will move forward cautiously through many "steps" under the guidance of their teacher. The suggested learning activities for this section are: 1. copying words or phrases; 2. copying sentences or paragraphs; and 3. writing from dictation. Exercises 2. and 3. are to be partially conducted in class under teacher's supervision.

WORDS IN CONTEXT

The vocabulary section comprises exercises in which the student must make considered lexical choices. Words are listed that are to be used to fill blanks in sentences. Where possible, an alternate word *(synonym),* or a phrase that explains the meaning, may be used to fill a particular slot. The finished sentences are further altered by *substitution, replacement,* or *transformation.*

STRUCTURES

Key words and phrases are expanded into complete sentences. This section also deals with groups of *adjectives-plus-preposition, verbs-plus-preposition,* and *nouns-plus-preposition* pairings that allow the student to generate new sentences.

GRAMMAR AND SYNTAX

Brief comments on the writing patterns and grammatical items contained in the *Model Composition* are made here. Further samples of writing are presented. These can be transformed by the student to express varying ideas, thus forcing production and encouraging the use of alternate vocabulary without altering syntactic structure. The student may supply all of the words on his vocabulary list that do not result in semantic absurdity.

IDEA RECOGNITION

Consideration is given here to the observation of logical syntac-

The student is encouraged to develop new *Patterns of Thought* following the "kernel idea" extracted from the *Model Composition*. This practice will extend the student's sense of productivity or creativity in writing.

VOCABULARY ENRICHMENT

To write effectively, the student learns new words. To retain these words, the student uses them repeatedly. In addition to providing the student with useful vocabulary, all exercises within this text are organized in a manner to stimulate the student to review and reuse the expressions already learned.

This section includes some helpful techniques for vocabulary expansion. One of the exercises used is *paraphrasing* the *Model Composition*. The student completes sentences by furnishing synonyms or equivalents of a given term, thereby becoming aware that there are frequently alternate ways of expressing roughly the same idea in English. A good exercise for the *paraphrasing* section is for the teacher to write the lines of the original narrative with the class writing the paraphrase.

Another helpful practice is the presentation of *lexical units,* i.e. words that may express related meanings through different structure.

Teacher: His *name* is Mark Anthony.
Student: They *call him* Mark Anthony.

Recognition of *related* words in context or in isolation may prove useful in building an active writing vocabulary. Related forms of *NOUNS, ADJECTIVES* and *VERBS* are requested here:

Example request for related *noun:*   Cue: *beautiful*
                                           Response: *beauty*

Example request for related *adjectives*:   Cue: *study*
                                             Response: *studious*

Example request for related *verb:*   Cue: *runner*
                                           Response: *run*

STEPS TO WRITING

At this point, the student will learn to rephrase excerpted model sentences by the *addition* or *deletion* of words and the revision of sentences. Small grammatical changes may also be necessitated in the process. Thus, if a model sentence reads, "He studies at the university," the assignment may call for changing "he" to "we." This change will require a substitution of "study" for "studies."

A variety of assignments related to those described above are used to force semi-independent production. This should ultimately lead to free writing.

COMPREHENSION

The comprehension exercises comprise a sequence of procedural steps. Some call for the completion of a statement by choosing phrases from the *Model Composition*. The student then adds sentences related in context. Further, the student answers questions requiring a clear understanding of ideas contained in the *Model Composition*. These are exercises that do not require either the production of sentences or the composition of statements.

COMMENTARY ON MODEL

The students are given key words or sentences from the *Model Composition*. They are to use these key expressions in their own composition on a topic related to that of the MODEL. Although the students may express agreement with the MODEL, they are encouraged to digress or disagree with the views of the model topic. This section constitutes partially guided writing; students are free to introduce an element of originality although they use known vocabulary and structures. As the students approach the final stages of the chapter, they should have enough "control" of the language to be able to manipulate what they have learned in order to express their own ideas and opinions.

COMPOSITION

At this point, the students are ready to be assigned a topic on which they will write a short composition. The extent of *Free Compo-*

sition is determined by the students' qualifications. The students may title the resulting composition with an appropriate heading.

Let's Continue

Phase Four: Let's Continue, is the final volume of the **English as a Second Language Series.** It is designed either for classroom use or for individual study with or without an instructor. The book is intended for students on the *Intermediate/ Advanced* level of their study of English. The text presupposes an already existing knowledge of basic grammar and verb usage. However, some chapters allow for the teaching or review of certain basic forms of grammar and syntax. It is aimed primarily at an adult college student, whether native English-speaking in need of supplementary study or a native of a foreign country wishing to advance to a higher level of English proficiency in an English speaking environment. However, utilizing its context appropriately, the text may also be found useful for the instruction of advanced level students of high-school age.

The primary objective of *Let's Continue* is to advance the student's comprehension and active expression in English, both spoken and written. The text will, therefore, undertake to present learning situations other than those usually encountered in the classroom. For that purpose, a variety of up-to-date readings have been composed. These will comprise stories, fairy tales, poems, news articles, songs (complete with music), cartoons, and graphics. Furthermore, all readings are accompanied, wherever necessary, by comprehensive marginal annotations which alleviate trouble spots.

It is noteworthy that the *annotations,* together with the *appendix* and a complete *active vocabulary* section, enable some students to use the book with little or no aid from an instructor. The book can just as easily, however, be used in a classroom situation.

Let's Continue is designed to help students of English as a Second Language improve their ability to understand and speak, read, write, and think in English. Every selection within the text, be it of serious or humorous nature, serves to encourage student comment and interpretation. The selections are, therefore, designed to appeal to student interests and be a sufficiently meaningful addition to the learning process in order to remain relevant in the days to come.

It is hoped that *Let's Continue* will enable students of English as a Second Language to extend their skills of English to greater complexity and sophistication. Though our concern here is to refine the student's usage of formal American English, primary importance is nevertheless given to extending the function of language as a means of everyday communication and expression.

Let's Continue is composed of ten (10) chapters. Each chapter comprises ten (10) sections; each section fulfills a specific task of instruction, i.e., it provides a learning "core" and various practice exercises in understanding, speaking, reading, writing, and grammatical reinforcement. All of the core presentations as well as the practice exercises which follow illustrate grammatical concepts in a systematic manner.

In addition, the previous proliferation of new vocabulary is presently brought under control; grammatical items learned in the initial *four phases* are treated further and new, more sophisticated, grammatical structures are introduced and expounded upon in depth. Writing exercises are both more numerous and more comprehensive; dialogues take on a more sophisticated level of comprehension. The use of grammar is only provided here as an aim to offer a wider knowledge of, and an increased competence in, the English language as a functional means of communication.

The material in each lesson is composed to appeal to a modern and universal individual. Some of the portions should inspire further discussion; others, i.e. the dialogues, might encourage practical participation and role playing in the classroom. The ultimate aim is to expand communicative skills. A few words about the chapter format are in order.

Each chapter is divided into ten (10) sections. Each section fulfills a specific function within the chapter.

It is advisable, therefore, that an attempt be made to complete them all. The flexibility of the presentation, however, allows the instructor or the student to select the order in which to proceed. The section approach makes it possible for the instructor or the student to determine precisely the order best suited to his/her needs.

The sections are as follows:

MODEL PRESENTATION

Each *Model Presentation*, be it in the form of dialogue, prose selection, poetry, song or other forms of written or oral communication, provides an introductory example for the new idiomatic and grammatical material within the chapter. Its contextual presentation is such that it will serve as the core of each lesson. Each subsequent section within the chapter is structured in reference to the core introduced material.

VOCABULARY

The vocabulary section comprises "special expressions" and words presented in the context of the *Model Presentation*. It serves as a means for vocabulary enrichment and practice in conversation as well as written expression. The special expressions will assist students in learning the meaning and usage of phrases commonly used in America.

CROSSWORD PUZZLES

This section further expands the student's knowledge of vocabulary. It allows a free association of expressions and the presentation of synonym-antonym relations in the context of the *Model Presentation*. All crossword puzzles comprise words taken from the *Model Presentation*.

GRAPHICS

The pictorial presentations of the situations comprising the *Model Presentation* help the student to better envision his/her role in its context. This makes for a more active, relevant participation and for an imaginative and meaningful retention of new expressions. Occasionally, songs may be presented here, both lyrics and music. They are to be sung in class.

GRAMMAR

This section presents grammatical analysis of the speech and writing items contained in the *Model Presentation*. Further samples are presented in varied context. An exercise section is included to serve the student in expressing varying ideas through transformation of the material learned. This type of exercise forces production and encourages the student to alternate vocabulary without changing syntactic structure. It is talking and writing intensive.

IDEA RECOGNITION

Emphasis is placed here on the recognition of logical syntactic and semantic relations within grammatically patterned sentences. The student is encouraged to develop further *thought Patterns* modeled on ideas from the *Model Presentation*.

VOCABULARY ENRICHMENT

Included are exercises based on patterns of speech, idioms, useful sayings, etc., all of which are helpful in the student's vocabulary expansion. Also, exercises in *paraphrasing* statements taken from the *Model Presentation* are included. The student becomes aware of alternate ways of expressing roughly the same idea in English. In fact, the expressions presented here are paraphrases of the original narrative; the student is to identify the paraphrased expressions in the *Model Presentation*.

STEPS IN CREATIVE EXPRESSION

At this point, the student learns to recreate the original *Model Presentation*. Given are multiple clues which the student must complete in order to achieve the goal of creating a coherent and logical unit of speech or writing. The exercises begin with small grammatical changes, such as "she" to "we" which in turn necessitate changes in verb structure from "goes" to "go," and then they introduce somewhat more sophisticated alterations, such as *lexical units* of structure changes, nouns to adjectives, to verbs, to adverbs, etc.

COMMENTARY ON MODEL PRESENTATION

The students are encouraged to think critically about the *Model Presentation*. They address a variety of criticisms, including questions which the students may answer straightforwardly or they may elaborate, presenting compositions of their own. These compositions are used for class recitation culminating in peer discussion and critical evaluation.

FREE COMPOSITION

At this point, the students are ready to be assigned various topics on which they will create short original presentations, imitating the forms of creative writing, found in the *Model Presentation*. Thus, the students may be assigned to compose a short narrative or a dialogue, write an essay or compose a poem, create a crossword puzzle, etc.

TEACHING SUGGESTIONS

LET'S BEGIN

All chapters in *Phase Zero Plus* begin with a preliminary foreword introducing terms and structures titled "In This Chapter."

It is not necessary to study this part of the chapter until later into the lesson. The chapter really begins with the composition titled "Situation." Students should be familiarized with this composition. Teacher reads sentences aloud; class repeats sentences. Explanation of vocabulary follows. More repetition by the entire class and by individual students. This helps students to reproduce distinctive sounds correctly.

The *"Dialogue"* is repeated by the entire class first. Individual repetition follows, after which the teacher assigns the different "roles" to individual students and asks them to read in front of the class. This may lead to a memorized dialogue presentation at the end of the lesson.

The *"Copy"* section is very important. Later in the book, this section of the chapter will be also called *"Listen"* and *"Write."* Initially, students copy words and expressions onto their notebooks. This exercise is especially useful for students whose native language is not written in the Roman alphabet.

The *"Repeat"* exercise is most useful when students study the names of the characters at first; later they cover the writing and identify the individuals by drawing alone. This exercise should be practiced intensively because it contributes to the understanding of simple courtesies in the American-English idiom.

Each section of *"Pronunciation Practice"* is to be drilled in the lab as well as in the classroom. It is important that students learn to pronounce the word before they go on to larger expressions and finally work up to the complete sentence. Using words in context will help students to understand their meaning and retain the vocabulary for future use.

Some time should be devoted to the section titled *Study*. Although less emphasis is placed in *Zero-Plus* on grammar than aural delivery, it is important to reinforce oral competence with correct structural habits. The *Study* section serves this purpose. Some of the more curious students will demand to know the "why's" and "what for's," and teachers should not dismiss this healthy curiosity lightly. On the whole, however, grammar is taught here deductively rather than inductively. It is constantly fed to the student through practical, functional use rather than by special emphasis.

It is important that all *Practice* exercises be done by the students and corrected in class while everyone can participate. Sentences should be pronounced aloud by the teacher and repeated aloud by students.

Example: (p. 27)

Teacher: I am a student. Students: I am a student

Teacher: Student:
She is a student. She is a student.
We are students. We are students.
etc.

Substitution Drills should be conducted in a similar fashion as the above.

Example: (p. 29)

Teacher: Hello, Hiromi.
Students: Hello Ann.
                  José.
                  Victoria
                  Isaac.

Complete, *Reading*, and *Talk* exercises on p. 30 should be done as homework, then corrected on the board in the classroom for all to see.

The *Guess Who* (p. 31) and *Give the Name* (p. 33) exercises should be conducted in class individually. These will prepare students to conduct a *Tell Your Friend* (p. 35) conversation as well as the section on *Writing.* (p. 36).

An added feature in all chapters is the *Proverb* at the end of each chapter. The teacher is to read the proverb then read the explanation in parentheses. Discussion is to follow, culminating in telling what "the drawings mean to me." Special emphasis should be given to complete coverage of the chapter. It is better to proceed slower and more thoroughly than go faster and miss establishing a solid foundation.

LET'S CONVERSE

All dialogues are presented in complete sentences, so that students learn all new words in a logical context. A student learning English must learn to hear and reproduce many distinctive sounds; vowels and consonants. For this purpose, as an initial presentation, it is suggested that you present one word at a time and build up to the complete utterance. The second section, *Words and Questions*, of each chapter lend themselves for such *warm-up* exercises. Students repeat sounds initially from open books. Later teacher may request that they cover the printed utterances. You may choose to point at the words written on the board or point to the item in an illustration. Have the class repeat words after you.

For example, in the sentences in Lesson 1 the teacher points to himself while saying "*My name is Mr. Lowell.*" Now point to the student and have class repeat "*Mary, Mary Alice Jefferson.*" Then point again at yourself and say "*I'm a teacher.*" Have the class repeat the statement. Then point to the student and say "*She's a student.*" Have the class repeat the statement. When the students have familiarized themselves sufficiently with the dialogue of Lesson 1, have small groups corresponding the numbers of persons in dialogue recreate the situation, first as in the dialogue itself, then in a personalized form.

Example: Instead of pointing at yourself and saying *"I'm Mr. Lowell,"* you may choose to give your own name, *"I'm Mr. Davis."* Then point to the student. Student will say *"I'm a student,"* *"My name is Linda Garcia,"* etc. etc.. Questions may follow statements, as in the practice sections, also on personalized basis as time goes on.

Dramatization and gestures can help to make the learning of vocabulary more interesting. Once students familiarize themselves with the new words, they can be called upon to read aloud utterances in the book. You must correct pronunciation errors immediately. Especial emphasis must be given to the pronunciation of cognates. Because of their similarity to the learner's native tongue they will be frequently mispronounced although their definition is clear. Repeat these cognates many times to give the learner an opportunity to use the word in isolation as well as in context.

The Chapters in *Let's Converse* follow a similar pattern throughout. The following general plan for presentation is suggested:

A. Teacher - pronounce the model dialogue; focus on vocabulary and go over the definitions presented in the test.

B. Students - repeat each word and phrase as a class then individually.

C. After you have presented the vocabulary and the students are familiar with all new words continue with the oral practices. This accomplished, you may proceed to explain the grammatical structures briefly before assigning the exercises under the heading of section Nine of the chapter.

D. To introduce new patterns have the students repeat the short Pronunciation Drill in unison two or three times. Then proceed to the following drill.

E. Special attention should be given the section under the heading *Vocabulary Building* which augments the usage of vocabulary previously learned. This section and the section of *Idioms*, may be studied simultaneously. These two sections lend themselves to an expansion of the usage of the words the learner has mastered in the dialogue section.

F. To help make drills more interesting, you may wish to draw simple drawings on the chalkboard, or dramatize the dialogue by having students act out the situations. This is especially useful once the conversation has been learned. Though the dialogues are brief, it is not recommended that they be memorized, however, this decision is left up to the instructor and may be modified to suit a variance of situations.

G. Once the dialogue has been thoroughly learned you may request individual students to describe the drawing at the beginning of the chapter. Finallly, divide class into small groups and give each an opportunity to dramatize the dialogue.

H. Make absolutely certain that the chapter has been mastered by the students before commencing with the following dialogue. Frequent review of covered material is the most useful way of testing progress.

LET'S READ

The reading selections, like the dialogues in *Let's Converse* contain only those structural or grammatical items which the students are about to learn or have already learned. In this way, the students are able to comprehend the reading selection without trying vainly to analyze and interpret structural forms as yet unlearned.

The reading selections are original creations which contain American English in its correct usage. The narratives center on occurrences in the lives of American families. They are followed by a unique exercise section called *Words in Context* or *Pictographs*, allowing the students to recreate the narrative from drawings, while also learning synonyms as well as the antonyms of new words used in the narrative. The pictures add a visual dimension to the narrative, while the added vocabulary expands the student's horizon for self-expression and improvisation. The topics themselves stimulate thought, imagination, and creativity.

The narratives are followed by a variety of comprehension exercises. It is preferable that these be done orally, but if the situation permits, they can be presented in written form. Vocabulary and narrative topics increase in sophistication as the students progress and their messages become more challenging than those of the initial compositions. The chapters also offer timed diagnostic vocabulary exercises as well as many others to amplify student's cognitive vocabulary for personalized use.

Reading material serves to reinforce oral comprehension. Reading selections offer students material for discussion and improvisation.

The study of the reading selection must be thorough if it is to serve as an incentive for oral discussion, Since all chapters follow a similar pattern of presentation, the following general plan of procedure is suggested:

A. Teacher explains the words given on introduction page and stresses the importance of learning the meanings of these key expressions. A more detailed explanation of each of the items will be given later in the *Grammar* section of the chapter.

B. Oral reading of narrative (paragraph by paragraph) — for vocalization, verbalization, pronunciation, and phrasing,

   1. Teacher: read the model; focus on sentence sense.

   2. Students: read first as a class then individually.

C. Silent reading (paragraph by paragraph) - for content and speed.

   1. Timing - the students are to look up when they finish reading each paragraph; note the time of first and of last student; evaluate later to establish average or explain norm.

   2. Comprehension - ask questions on content using
      a) yes/no type questions
      b) interrogatives as follows if applicable:
         what
         who / whom
         where

when
how
why

D. Exercises

1. Words in Context
    a) Make the students look up the words in the narrative, read sentences aloud, and try to guess meaning in context.
    b) Check with book's answers only if students could not guess.
    c) Have students use the same words in their own sentences.

2. Perform the rest of the exercises on
    a) filling the blanks with missing words or phrases according to the narrative-word recognition, concept, synonym/antonym, and with the most appropriate words to complete meaning.

3. Comprehension
    a) logical and structural sequence
    b) true or false
    c) matching two parts of same sentence

4. On grammatical aspects
    a) Teacher: present and illustrate the grammar point of lesson.
    b) Students: underline in the narrative the grammar point, for content and structural recognition and application.

5. Oral and written composition can be based or patterned on or similar to narrative; it can be personal and original.

6. Study *Poem* and discuss for meaning allowing students time to learn supplementary vocabulary.

7. Testing
    a) Questions on comprehension

b) On vocabulary - patterned after any one of the exercises or vocabulary drills.

c) On sentence patterns based on matching two parts or numbering logical sequences of thoughts.

8. Create original sentences to illustrate grammar point.

9. Transparencies of the drawings in the chapter are shown and students recreate the narrative from memory.

LET'S WRITE

The book is divided into three sections beginning with Chapter Two. The sections deal with writing the *"sentence,"* the *"paragraph,"* and writing the *composition.* Preceeding the three main sections is Chapter One which introduces the *Word*, its construction, background, development, etc.. Since all knowledge of written as well as oral communication is primarily based on a 55 sound vocabulary foundation, it is suggested that special attention be given Chapter One before embarking on subsequent study.

Chapters Two through Ten follow much the same pattern of presentation. You will note that each chapter introduces a new aspect of grammatical structure. The *"Model"* compositions are original, and comprise various types of formal and informal writing ranging from a simple sentence to a model term paper.

The following general plan of procedure is suggested:

A.Teacher reads *Model* composition aloud while students follow silently with books open.

B. Students perform the reading in unison and individually.

C. Once the entire *Model* has been presented, you may wish to call on students to give an oral review. You may make up questions to facilitate the review. Such reviews should be done in class to avoid having the students memorize written material at home.

D. Once the *Model* is learned, conduct a question and answer session with students asking questions of one another under teacher's supervision. It is recommended that the student not be interrupted for corrections of slight grammatical or structural errors. However, this is left up to the discretion of the teacher.

E. Go over definitions of words and phrases in class before proceeding with the copying exercises of I., B. *Composition by Degree.*

F. Follow each of the exercise sections in the chapter, stressing those points which seem more important in your particular situation. The selection of points of emphasis will vary and is left up to the discretion of the teacher.

G. Arriving at the final stages of the chapter, students should be able to reproduce whole selections and write them in a clear manner with minimum mistakes in spelling or grammar. A good way to help students get ready for free composition is to diagnose individual problems. The teacher must work with students as a group and individually to inspire in them the confidence they need for free composition.

LET'S CONTINUE

This is the last book of the *ESL LET'S* SERIES. As such, it is a compliment to the entire series. It deals with grammatical and structural items of American English not previously discussed and learned. It also introduces words of greater sophistication (low and high frequency), with which students may not be familiar, i.e. two-word verbs, compound prepositions, etc.

The chapters of *Let's Continue* present situations that allow for breaching the gap between the classroom and the real world. They offer material which affords much interaction, such as a shopping trip to the grocery or asking for directions in a city and finding the proper places on the map.

All ten chapters follow much the same pattern of presentation. The chapters are divided into ten sections, each section fulfilling a specific function within the learning process. These sections are all described in the *Preface*. I suggest that you study them thoroughly before going into the classroom situation. A well prepared teacher will motivate students to reach greater heights in their learning process. The following general plan of procedure is suggested:

A. Teacher reads the *Words to Remember,* explaining each new words. Write new word on the board, pronounce aloud and let class repeat. Explain word in context; make up a sentence to suit the situation in the chapter.

B. Proceed to pronounce words and their synonyms on the margins of the *ModelPresentations*. Make sure everyone is familiarized with the new words.

C. Read *Dialogue* aloud. First follow up with choral then individual repetition. Students may act out each role of the *Dialogue*.

D. Read *Narrative* aloud. Have students read aloud and discuss points with which they are not familiar. Allow for questions and answers. Always interrupt class proceedings to ask "are there any questions?"

E. Have students discuss the *Narrative"* in class. If it is a large class, divide students into small discussion groups and allow time for discussion. At an assigned time, each group "leader" will report the subjects discussed to the entire class. More class discussion to follow. Such discussion sessions need constant teacher participation in order not to run out of control.

F. Assign homework which is to be checked and discussed in class. All exercises requiring oral repetition are on tape and should be practiced in the lab as well as in the classroom.

G. Students describe the pictures and offer their comments for discussion in class. Teacher picks up all homework, corrects and grades it before returning it to the students.

H.*Crossword Puzzle* and *Song* are usually conducted in class. Each chapter's CD and cassette recording of the oral exercises also contains a piano rendition of the song. Teacher explains the new words contained in the song, then students sing to the accompaniment of the recording. Sometimes, there is a musically talented student in class who can accompany the singing on a guitar or another instrument. Have class participation.

I. *Grammar* is only explained on request. The *Practice* exercises should be conducted in class, with the use of the board.

J. All exercises are to be assigned as homework, to be presented in class, corrected by the teacher and returned to the students.

K.The *Vignette* is an added feature. It should be studied thoroughly and new words explained by the teacher. All *Vignettes* deal with life in the United States and offer foreign students an intimate glimpse at the daily life in this country. *Questions* for *Discussion* follow the *Vignette*. Time should be devoted to discussion and explanations much like the procedure of the *Narrative*.

L. Beginning with *Free Composition*, on to the *"Fill in the Missing Dialogue"* can serve as an evaluative procedure for the entire chapter and should be assigned as homework. *Commentary on the Model* should be assigned in the form of a paragraph composition or more to be corrected by the teacher and returned to the students.

SAMPLE LESSON PLANS
WITH SUGGESTED TIMEKEEPER

In response to our questionnaire concerning the number of hours per week devoted to the basic ESL course, a majority indicated four hours. Some responses indicated, however, that classes met three hours weekly and others said that classes met five hours weekly.

As a cross-section of the above allocations, we recommend that five sessions be devoted to each lesson; the sixth to be a review and evaluation test.

Following are five sample daily lesson plans. They are to serve as guides, knowing that each individual group, or class, must progress at a rate that is realistic for the particular group and learning situation.

A. Lesson Plan—*Let's Begin*, Chapter Three
"See you at 7 o'clock"

Structures Studied: Possessive Adjectives,
my/your/his/her/our/our/their
Present Continuous of Verbs - be & Verb + ing
Numbers 0 (zero) to 20 (twenty)
Telling time:
when?/early/late/on time/always/never/today/o'clock

Time Period: Classroom periods of fifty minutes each.

lst Day

Warm-up reading aloud the *Situation* (10 min.). Students repeat.

1. Explain new words. Read aloud in context, etc.
2. Pronounce *Dialogue* (10 min.). - Explain new words.
    Students repeat together.
3. Students read *Situation* individually (15 min.).
4. Students read *Dialogue* individually (15 min.).

2nd Day

1. Warm-up reading *Situation* (5 min.).
2. Warm-up reading *Dialogue* (5 min.).
3. Students read *Situation*. Ask questions (10 min.).
4. Students play roles of *Dialogue* (20 min.).
5. Copy (10 min.).

3rd Day

1. Copy (10 min.).
2. Pronunciation Practice. Teacher and class repeats
    (20 min).
3. Pronunciation Practice. Students practice individually
    (10 min).
4. Pronunciation Practice. Teacher repeats alone (10 min).

4th Day

Grammar presentation: Affirmative-Negative (15 min.)
                        Questions and Answers (20 min.)
                        Possessive Adjectives (15 min.)

5th Day
1. Review of 4th Day presentation (5 min.)
2. *Grammar* presentation: Present Continuous (15 min.)
                        Numbers (10 min.)
                        Telling time (10 min.)
                        Counting (10 min.)

6th Day

1. Quiz on Material covered previous 5 days (20 min.).
2. Exercises on *Grammar* thus far covered. (30 min.).

B. Lesson Plan—*Let's Converse,* Chapter Six
"Getting a Job"

Structures Studied: Present perfect tense, irregular past and past participle, expressions with the verb *get*, adverbials of frequency (frequency words).

Time Period: Classroom periods of fifty minutes each.

1st Day

Warm-up (5 min.).
1. Informal conversation; questions to instructor; review questions (10 min.)
2. Presentation of half of dialogue, use of transparency; answer questions on vocabulary and punctuation (10 min.)
3. Questions to students about dialogue, what happens in it (5 min.)
4. Grammar presentation: present perfect tense (5 min.)
5. Speakers: (10 min.)
6. Activity (5 min.)

2nd Day

Warm-up (5 min.): V, *Statements*
1. Informal conversation (10 min.)
2. Review of grammar transparencies; questions from students (5 min.); finish dialogue
3. Presentation of irregular past participles (pp. 145-147), (5 min.)
4. Practice: A, 1, 2, 3; *Yes and No* Exercises: 1, 1, 2, 3 (10 min.)
5. Historical anecdote, questions for comprehension (10 min.)
6. Activity (5 min.)

3rd Day

Warm-up: *Get* expressions, p. 144 (5 min.)
1. Practice: A, 4 (p. 156); Exercises: A, 4 (10 min.)
2. Conversation: B (10 min.)

3. Board work: sentences (p. 139), A, Word usage (p. 144) (10 min.); discussion
4. Groups: Practice situation presented in dialogue (10 min.)
5. Activity (5 min.)

4th Day

Warm-up (5 min.)
1. Presentation of adverbials of frequency, pp. 147-148 (5 min.)
2. Practice: B, C (pp152-153); Exercises: B, C (pp 157-158) (15 min.)
3. Group work: Continue practicing dialogue situation (10 min.)
4. Conversation: B, C (p. 160) (10 min.)
5. Activity (5 min.)

5th Day

Warm-up (5 min.)
1. Informal questions (5 min.)
2. Grammar review (5 min.)
3. Group presentations of dialogue situation; correct for grammar and pronunciation (15 min.)
4. Comprehension tape and questions and/or simple test (10 min.)
5. Activity: Slides, music, game, etc. (10 min.)

6th Day

1. Quiz on Chapter Six (both written and oral).
2. Begin new chapter.

C. Lesson Plan—*Let's Read*, Chapter Two
"A Weekend in the Country"

Time Period: Classroom periods of fifty minutes each.

1st Day

1. Explanation of words on introduction page of chapter

given. Stress the importance of learning the meaning of these words. More detailed explanation of the items given later (10 min.).

2. Students read narrative aloud in class. As many students as possible are given a chance to read. Corrections are made for any mispronounced words (15 min.).

3. Students asked to give their reactions to the story and discuss the meaning of any sentence they do not understand (10 min.).

4. *Words in Context (Pictographs)* pronounced by instructor. Questions made as to the meanings of the words. Then, sentences are made according to instructions given in the text. All students are encouraged to participate in this portion of the lesson. I feel it is one of the most beneficial portions of the lesson (10 min.).

5. Homework given for next day. (Included Section B of Four *Sentences* on page 28 and a review of story and vocabulary
(5 min.).

2nd Day

1. Homework taken up, and class is opened to questions regarding such (5 min.).

2. Three *Structures* (*Phrases*) exercise completed in class. Instructor writes sentences on the blackboard. Errors in sentence construction are pointed out (15 min.).

3. *Grammar* and *Syntax* (*Points* of *Interest*) discussed in class. Definition and examples of entire section given. Then, students are called upon to give their own examples, which they write on the blackboard (20 min.).

4. Exercise A, Four, Sentences pages 28-29 are completed in class (5 min.).

5. Homework assignments given - *Word Recognition* pages 31, 33 A & B (5 min.)

3rd Day

1. *Word Recognition* pages 31-33 A & B discussed in class (10 min.).

NOTE: FOR ALL EXERCISES STUDENTS READ

SENTENCES ALOUD AND CORRECTIONS ARE
MADE AS SUGGESTED.
2. *Concept Recognition* Seven, pages 34-36 (20 min.).
3. *Telling* the *Meaning* Exercises A, B, and C (15 min.).
4. Homework assignments given: *Comprehension* (Exercises)
A & B pages 40-45 (5 min.).

4th Day

1. Homework taken up and discussed (15 min.).
2. *Comprehension* (Exercise) C, page 45 (15 min.).
3. *Composition* and *Discussion* A completed (15 min.).
4. Homework assignments given - *Composition* and *Discussion* B (5 min.).

5th Day

1. *Composition* and *Discussion* B (10 min.).
2. *Composition* and *Discussion* C completed, allowing all
students a chance to participate in using vocabulary learned
(10 min.).
3. Instructor reads *Poem*, Exercise D, page 48. Explanations
given of footnotes and questions are answered. Usually,
this section interests students because of the unusual usage of words in poetry, and the different meanings the
poem has for different people. Time spent on this section
depends on the poem and the type of information that
must be located regarding the grammar (20 min.).
4. Brief review of grammar introduced in the chapter, and
class opened for final discussion of vocabulary introduced
in that chapter. Assignment given for next day - Read
Chapter Three and study second section, *Words* in *Context*, on pages 51, 52, and 53. Students are asked to have
any questions ready for discussion regarding narrative and
vocabulary usage (10 min.).

6th Day

1. Quiz given on Chapter Two.
2. Begin new chapter.

D. Lesson Plan—*Let's Write*, Chapter Two "The Simple Sentence"

lst Day

1. Discussion by instructor of the grammar notes (simple sentence, subject/verb relationship, kinds of sentences, punctuation of sentence, six basic tenses). Definition of all terms explained and examples are written on blackboard. Students are then required to produce examples of their own. Handout given to students on verbs (subject/verb relationship and six basic tenses) (40 min.).
2. *Model Composition* read by instructor, and then discussed by the class. Homework assignment given - Pages 35-36 *Composition* by *Degrees*, and *Structures* Three, pages 39-41 (10 min.).

2nd Day

1. Questions asked about *Model Composition* (5 min.).
2. Pages 36 and 37 completed orally in class by students. Answers placed on blackboard by instructor (15 min.).
3. Page 40-41, exercise B (preposition) completed in class orally. Teacher repeats alone (10 min).
4. Exercise E Pages 47-50 completed in class. (numbers 1, 2, 3, & 4) (15 min.).
5. Homework assignment given: Page 50 Exercise E, number 5 (punctuation), *Idea Recognition* Page 50, and *Vocabulary Enrichment* Page 51 (5 min.).

3rd Day

1. Page 52 *Lexical Units* B and *Related Words* C completed in class by students orally (15 min.).
2. Page 53 *Steps in Writing* and Page 53 *Opposites* completed in class (15 min.).
3. Pages 54 and 55 *Comprehension* completed in class orally (10 min.).
4. Students required to write ten simple sentences of their

own and Homework assignment given: Pages 55-56 *Composition* A & B (10 min.).

4th Day

1. Page 55 Nine, *Commentary* on Model A & B (15 min.).
2. Page 55 Ten, discussion of free composition based on *Model Composition*, to be done at home. All phrases explained and reviewed (20 min.).
3. Rewriting of section Ten, B. in class. Work taken up by teacher for correction (to be returned next day) (15 min.).

5th Day

1. Homework of section Ten, B. returned to students and discussed. *Composition* picked up by teacher (20 min.).
2. Brief review of grammar notes and class opened up for questions on chapter. Assignment for next class given (30 min.).

6th Day

1. Quiz given on Chapter Two.
2. Begin new chapter.

E. Lesson Plan—*Let's Continue,* Chapter Two "At the Dentist's"

lst Day

1. Discuss two-word verbs and explain new words (15 min.).
2. Explain marginal words of *Dialogue* (20 min.).
3. Pronounce *Dialogue* (15 min.).

2nd Day

1. Pronounce *Dialogue.* Class repeats (15 min.).
2. Students pronounce individually (35 min.).

3rd Day

1. Bring to class pictures of scenes related to the *Dialogue* that you and your students could talk about. Find some pictures of things that dentists do. Read *Dialogue* individually. Present the pictures. Write the words to be used on the board, like *teeth, cavities, care,* etc.
2. In addition, find pictures of things that dentists do *not* do (e.g. sell furniture, install T.V. sets, etc.) and do the same with these pictures.
3. Say to your class, "This is a picture of a dentist. What do dentists do?" and have students find the picture and words telling something dentists do. When students select the right picture, ask "What else does the dentist do?"
4. Continue with question and answer game concerning the activities of the dentist. Have students ask each other such questions. (50 minutes)

4th Day

1. Review previous lessons (20 min.).
2. Pronounce and explain vocabulary of *Narrative* (30 min.).

5th Day

1. Read *Narrative* (30 min.).
2. Discuss *Narrative* (20 min.).

6th Day

1. Review of material covered thus far (20 min.).
2. Evaluation of material covered (30 min.).

INTRODUCTION TO TESTING
AND EVALUATION

There is always a need to assess language proficiency; a need to measure the complete range of language competence from the skill acquired in elementary courses to that reflecting more advanced study, all the way to reaching near native facility. It is especially important to evaluate this process of language learning of someone who has progressed from "Zero" knowledge to the point when English has become his/her principal language of communication.

A proficiency evaluation (some call it "test" or "examination"), is an attempt to probe the examinee's functional competence in the language and to make him/her aware of both their capacities and limitations. Evaluation results have specific meaning in terms of what the examinee can accomplish; they measure the examinee's language proficiency.

In order to measure the student's language performance, all evaluation tools before and after instruction are constructed similar in format though differing in content; they test precisely the skills and vocabulary which the student should have learned within the span of learning.

The EVALUATIONS that follow are samples prepared and administered in the classroom during a semester's work. All these samples should serve as models which can be duplicated or modified to suit a given situation. It should be remembered that classroom situations are different in most cases, although the learning material may be the same. The volume, the degree of difficulty of the material tested, and the total testing time may differ in most cases. Above all, progress and achievement should be observed and evaluated often so as to maintain a current picture of the students' capabilities as well as a close scrutiny of the teacher's effectiveness. It is imperative to place students at their level of competence at the very outset of their language studies. The sample placement evaluations may be used in their present form or modified to suit a specific situation. It is also important to evaluate students on individual achievement rather than by comparison to other students. It is, therefore, advisable to test according to the student's personal degree of achievement.

To become an effective tool of the total learning process, student EVALUATION must be frequent, fair, and serve as a self-evaluation of teacher-effectiveness; a kind of professional accountability.

The evaluation of progress made in the classroom is a vital part of teaching. The teacher's role as judge of the effectiveness of instruction and progress of the students can not and should not be underestimated.

There are innumerable ways to test the various aspects of progress made in class. Many types of tests have been created for this purpose, which the limited space here does not permit us to include. The texts of this LET'S SERIES of ESL is designed in such a manner as to render valuable assistance to the teacher in administering evaluative tests to his/her students. Many sections of our chapters are in fact designed for the dual purpose of instructing and testing.

We have included here many sample tests, some are for the indicated chapters, others to be used at will. Samples are given for pre-testing, progress evaluation, and for achievement.

ELEMENTARY PLACEMENT EVALUATION
(SPELLING)

Directions: In each of the following groups of words, one is spelled correctly. Place the letter of the correct answer in the space provided on the left. Example:

_____ 0.

a. foreign
b. forign   You should have put "a" — foreign
c. foregn
d. farign

_____ 1 .

a. believe
b. bilive
c. beilive
d. beliv

_____ 2.

a. backward
b. bakward
c. bacward
d. beckward

_____ 3.

a. becouse
b. bekus
c. bekause
d. because

_____ 4.

a. payd
b. payed
c. paid
d. peid

_____ 5.

a. rison
b. reason
c. reazon
d. raison

_____ 6.

a. accomodate
b. acomodate
c. accommodate
d. akomodate

_____ 7.

a. anxziety
b. anxiety
c. anziety
d. angziety

_____ 8.

a. bulletin
b. buletin
c. buetin
d. bolletin

_____ 9.

a. comittee
b. commitee
c. committe
d. committee

_____ 10.

a. college
b. colege
c. kollege
d. colleg

_____ 11.

a. disipline
b. discipline
c. dicipline
d. dosciplin

_____ 12.

a. efficient
b. aficient
c. efficiant
d. ifficient

_____ 13.

a. especialy
b. ispecially
c. especially
d. especilly

_____ 14.

a. government
b. goverment
c. governent
d. governmente

_____ 15.

a. handkerchif
b. handcerchief
c. hankerchief
d. handkerchief

_____ 16.

a. labratory
b. laboratory
c. lebratory
d. labortori

_____ 17.

a. medicine
b. medisine
c. medicin
d. medacine

_____ 18.

a. planing
b. planning
c. plannin
d. planin

_____ 19.

a. temprature
b. temperatur
c. temperature
d. temperture

_____ 20.

a. prefired
b. preferd
c. prefered
d. preferred

ELEMENTARY PLACEMENT EVALUATION
(ORAL COMPREHENSION)

This evaluation may be administered by the instructor or done in pairs by the students themselves under instructor's supervision. Instructor grades end result of both kinds of evaluations.

1.   Hello, my name is _____.What's yours? How do you spell your name?

2.   Do you speak English?

3.   Do you think English is easy?

4.   How long are you here in the U.S.?

5.   Where do you come from?

6.   Do you like it here in _____ ?

7.   What do you do every day?

8.   What do you like to do on weekends?

9.   Do you have a hobby?

10.   Do you like sports?

11.   What do you like to do the most?

12.   Is your family here?

13.   Where does your family live?

14.   What does your father do for a living?

15.   Do you have any brothers and sisters?

16.   How old are your siblings? (brothers and sisters)

17.   How do you like this city?

18.   Do you have many friends?

19.   Are your friends American?

20.   What did you do yesterday?

21.   What was the weather like?

22.   Does it rain much in your country?

23.   Do you have snow in the winter?

24.   Why did you come to this country?

25.   What is it that you like most about the U.S.?

26.   Have you been at this college (university) before?

27.   Who told you about this college (university)?

28.   Did you have any difficulty being admitted?

29.   Did you study English before?

30.   Where did you complete High School?

31.   What are you going to study in this country?

32.   Who is helping you through college?

33.   Have you visited other countries?

34.   What do you like to see in this country?

35.   What don't you like about this country?

36.   Where do you live now?

37.   How do you get to school?

38.   Is the traffic heavy?

39.   Do you take a bus or do you drive?

40.   What kind of transportation do you like the most?

41.   How do people travel in your country?

42.   Are you having difficulty communicating with people?

43.   Do you think people are friendly in the U.S.?

44.   Do you have a "best friend?"

45.   Please describe your friend.

46.   Tell us something about your family.

47.   Tell us something about your town or city.

48.   How would you go about getting a hotel room?

49.   How would you go about buying a car?

50.   I have a problem; I can't get up early in the mornings. Tell me what I can do to be on time at work.

ELEMENTARY PLACEMENT EVALUATION
(WRITING)

Select a, b, c, or d to complete sentence.

___ 1.   That's _____ eraser.

a. a   c. in
b. an   d. on

___ 2.   notebook/be/this/whose _____?

a. Is whose notebook this?   c. Notebook whose is this?
b. Whose notebook is this?   d. Whose notebook be this?

___ 3.   There's the _____ _____

a. red car   c. car green
b. car red   d. car small

___ 4.   1 student, 2 _____

a. studentes   c. students
b. student   d. studint

___ 5.   1 man, 2 _____

a. mans   c. men
b. manes   d. mean

___ 6.   1 housewife, 2 _____

a. housewives   c. housewife
b. yousewifs   d. housevive

59

___7.   _____ are friendly.

a. Mexicans   c. an Mexicans
b. The Mexicans   d. a Mexicans

___ 8.   Mr. Lee is _____ the classroom.

a. in   c. above
b. on   d. at

___ 9.   John_____good.

a. is   c. am
b. are   d. ain't

___ 10.   Hiromi and José _____friends?

a. do are   c. are
b. do is   d. is

___ 11.   _____one book on the table.

a. there is   c. is
b. there are   d. are

___ 12.   What are those? _____oranges.

a. it's   c. there are
b. they're   d. they is

___ 13.   Is Mr. Carson a lawyer?

a. Yes, she's a lawyer.   c. No, its; not a lawyer
b. No, she's not a lawyer.   d. No, he's not a lawyer.

___ 14.   Where is Isaac? Isaac _____.

a. is good   c. is stupid
b. is at home   d. is a lawyer

___ 15. What are you doing? _____.

a. I'm home   c I'm eating
b. I don't eat   d. I eating

___16. Are the men building the bridge? No, they _____ the bridge.
a. are   c. aren't building
b. are building   d. building

___17. Yukio, tell Pedro not to close the door. Yukio: "Pedro, _____the door."

a. close   c. don't close
b. no close   d. close not

___18. The teacher_____English.

a. speak   c. don't speak
b. speaks   d. do speak

___19. _____ speak/the teacher/English?

a. do the speak   c. does the teacher speak
b. don't the teacher speak d. speaks the teacher

___20. What time does he go to the store? _____.

a. he go at 9 o'clock   c. John goes
b. he goes at 9 o'clock   d. no he goes home

___21. Angel studies the lesson.
      No, Angel_____the lesson.

a. doesn't study   c. don't study
b. that's Angel's   d. that Angel

___22. Whose book is that? _____book

a. that's Berthas'   c. that's of Bertha
b. that's Bertha's   d. that Bertha

___ 23. What are they going to do? _____.

a.   They're going to eat   c. they going to eat
b.   they eat   d. they not eat

___ 24. Where are you _____?

a. from   c. near
b. to   d. about

___25. Do they live _____ the Carsons?

a. to   c. during
b. near   d. for

___26. When does he take care _____ the yard?
a. at   c. in
b. of   d. about

___27. What time does he arrive _____the office?

a. of   c. about
b. in   d. at

___28. Do you work? No, _____.

a. I don't   c. he doesn't
b. I do   d. He don't

___29. Are they good? Yes, _____.

a. they're   c. they are
b. they is   d. they aren't

___30. Mrs. Naga is going ___ the store.

a. in   c. at
b. on   d. to

____ 31. A small child _____ walk.

a. do   c. don't
b. can   d. ink

____ 32.   The bread; a _____.

a. I bread   c. bread piece
b. piece of bread   d. little bread

____ 33.   Do you have _____ apples?

a. some   c. a
b. any   d. to

____ 34.   No, I haven't _____ cream.

a. some   c. a
b. any   d. to

____ 35. How much money does he have? He_____ .

a. have a house   c. has two cars
b. has $5.00   d. have three pigs

____ 36. The Carsons ____ tired last night.

a. was   c. is
b. were   d. are

____37. Mrs. Jones ____ tired last night.

a. were   c. is
b. was   d. are

____ 38.   I _____ a lot yesterday.

a.   work   c. working
b.   worked   d. worket

____ 39. Alice writes the letter today. Last week she _____ the letter.

a. wrote   c. writed
b. wroted   d. write

___40. Did they go to Acapulco? No, they _____.

a. did go   c. didn't go
b. don't go   d. went

___41. Did he wear his raincoat? Yes, he _____ his raincoat.

a. weared   c. wore't go
b. weird   d. wore

___42. Did they hold the meeting? Yes, they ____ the meeting.

a.   holded   c. held
b.   hilded   d. had

___43. Whose book is that? (me) _____book.

a.   that me   c. that's my
b.   that's me   d. that's mine

___44.   Is it Jane's room? Yes, it's _____ .

a.   hers   c. theirs
b.   his   d. their

___45.   Does Mrs. Dawson drive the car? Yes, she drives _____ .

a.   it   c. they
b.   its   d. them

___46.   Do you like those people? Yes, I like _____.

a.   it   c. its
b.   they   d. them

___47. Please _____the numbers from one to twenty.

a. get   c. said
b. tell   d. told

___48. I have a present _____.

a. them   c. for them
b.. be them   d. to them

___49. Joe is _____than John.

a. tall   c. tallest
b. taller   d. more tall

___50. Friends are _____ than money.

a. importanter   c. important
b. more important   d. weird

INTERMEDIATE DIAGNOSTIC
VOCABULARY EVALUATION

The purpose of this test is to obtain an estimate of the student's proficiency in English in terms of the size of his/her vocabulary. The words included in this test include one word for each frequency category from 50 or more down to one per million words of reading matter, as reported in Thorndike and Lorge, *Teacher's 30,000 Word Book*. Words which obviously changed frequency of usage since this book was published were eliminated from the test.

The student's vocabulary size may be estimated from his test score (1 to 50) as follows:

Score	Words	Score	Words	Score	Words	Score	Words	Score	Words
1	2021	11	2397	21	2963	31	3886	41	6093
2	2057	12	2438	22	3037	32	4018	42	6534
3	2092	13	2485	23	3114	33	4163	43	7056
4	2125	14	2535	24	3202	34	4335	44	7640
5	2163	15	2598	25	3278	35	4523	45	8333
6	2205	16	2651	26	3363	36	4712	46	9223
7	2243	17	2715	27	3435	37	4912	47	10287
8	2282	18	2770	28	3533	38	5143	48	11729
9	2312	19	2835	29	3743	39	5437	49	14232
10	2352	20	2889	30	3755	40	5753	50	19441

This test is to help us to know the level of your ability in English. It does not count on your grade. Take your time. If you do not know an answer, do not try to guess. Skip on to the next question. The first questions are easiest.

Choose the correct answer for each question.

For example:

An <u>author</u> _____.

a. sings   b. cooks   c. dances   d. writes

"d. writes" is correct. Therefore place "<u>d</u>" in the space provided.

- -

1. <u>Magazines</u> are used to _____.
   a. drink   b. eat   c. read   d. write

2. A <u>navy</u> must have _____.
   a. cars   b. jeeps   c. ships   b. tanks

3. A <u>neighborhood</u> is those who live _____.
   a. in the same block   b. far away
   c. in another town   d. in another state

4. A <u>meadow</u> is a place where farm animals eat _____.
   a. bread   b. cookies   c. grass   d. meat

5. A <u>mirror</u> is used to see _____.
   a. the ground   b. oneself   c. the sea   d. the sky

6. A <u>painting</u> is done by _____.
   a. an artist   b. a musician   c. a plumber   d. a writer

7. The <u>midst</u> is _____.
   a. in the center   b. at the edge
   c. at the side   d. at the top

8. The <u>operator</u> of a car _____.
   a. cleans it   b. drives it   c. repairs it   d. rides in

9. A <u>mystery</u> is something that is _____.
   a. known   b. seen   c. understood   d. unknown

10. A <u>person</u> has _____.
   a. one tail   b. two eyes   c. three hands   d. four knees

11. A <u>pencil</u> is used to _____.
   a. hear   b. read   c. speak   d. write

12. A <u>mixture</u> is _____.
   a. coffee and cream   b. salt   c. sugar   d. water

13. <u>Marble</u> is _____.
   a. gas   b. liquid   c. hard   d. soft

14. A <u>mayor</u> is head of a _____.
   a. city   b. county   c. state   d. nation

15. <u>Moreover</u> means _____.
   a. although   b. however   c. in addition   d. nevertheless

16. <u>Muscles</u> are used to _____.
   a. rest   b. think   c. understand   d. work

17. A <u>mouse</u> is _____.
   a. an animal   b. a bird   c. a bug   d. a fish

18. A <u>marvelous</u> thing is _____.
   a. common   b. great   c. ordinary   d. unimportant

19. <u>Mild</u> weather is _____.
   a. hot   b. fair   c. rainy   d. windy

20. <u>Humankind</u> is _____.
   a. birds   b. bugs   c. people   d. plants

21. A <u>messenger</u> brings _____.
    a. clothing   b. food   c. information   d. money

22. A <u>moderate</u> speed is _____.
    a. fast   b. slow
    c. not too fast, not too slow   d. changeable

23. People <u>mourn</u> _____.
    a. at Christmas   b. at birthdays
    c. at weddings   d. at funerals

24. Good <u>management</u> in business brings _____.
    a. complaints   b. losses   c. problems   d. profits

25. If a person <u>maintains</u> a car, he _____.
    a. checks it regularly   b. junks it
    c. makes it   d. repairs it

26. An <u>onion</u> is a kind of _____.
    a. animal   b. bird   c.mineral   d. plant

27. If a person <u>multiplies</u> 2 times 3, the result is _____.
    a. 4   b. 5   c. 6   d. 7

28. A <u>medium</u> sized person is _____.
    a. fat   b. tall   c. wide   d. none of these

29. The <u>mission</u> of the army is to _____.
    a. build buildings   b. enlist people
    c. get guns   d. protect the country

30. A <u>menace</u> is _____.
    a. black   b. dangerous   c. heavy   d. round

31. A <u>mob</u> has _____.
    a. one person   b. two people
    c. a few people   d. many people

32. A <u>minor</u> detail is _____.
    a. complicated   b. large   c. permanent   d. unimportant

33. A <u>mansion</u> is a house which is _____.
    a. large   b. middle sized   c. small   d. red

34. A <u>mask</u> is worn on the _____.
    a. face   b. feet   c. hands   d. waist

35. A <u>mechanic</u> works on _____.
    a. doors   b. motors   c. seats   d. windows

36. A person is <u>mistaken</u> if he/she thinks that the earth is _____.
    a. flat   b. round   c. a planet   d. solid

37. A <u>magistrate</u> is a _____.
    a. doctor   b. judge   priest   d. teacher

38. A <u>toddler</u> is a _____.
    a. squirrel   b. bird   c. child   d. toy

39. A <u>meter</u> is used to _____.
    a. read   b. write   c. measure   d. draw

40. A <u>massive</u> animal is _____.
    a. black   b. large   c. round   d. square

41. A <u>mattress</u> is used for _____.
    a. eating   b. drinking   c. reading   d. sleeping

42. In her <u>make-up</u>, a woman uses _____.
    a. books   b. lip stick   c. mustard   d. pens

43. A <u>marginal</u> salary is _____.
    a. a large amount   b. an average amount
    c. a huge amount   d. barely enough

44. a <u>manger</u> is a place to keep _____.
    a. books   b. dishes   c. hay   d. water

45. An example of a <u>mammal</u> is a _____.
    a. cow   b. duck   c. snake   d. spider

46. <u>Mahogany</u> is a kind of _____.
    a. cloth   b. metal   c. stone   d. wood

47. To be <u>mindful</u> is to _____.
    a. forget   b. neglect   c. reject   d. think

48. <u>Magnesium</u> is _____.
    a. an animal   b. a flower   c. a bird   d. a metal

49. A <u>mania</u> is _____.
    a. depressive   b. logical   c. planned   d. uncontrolable

50. A <u>mackerel</u> is a kind of _____.
    a. animal   b. fish   c. mineral   d. vegetable

INTERMEDIATE PLACEMENT
EVALUATION

PART ONE: DISCRIMINATION

Indicate on the line provided on the left which letter (a., b., c., or d.) best completes the sentence. Fill in the sentence.

____1. Go into the classroom. The teacher _____ your name.

    a. call
    b. calls
    c. calling
    d. is calling

____2. _____ Fred _____ when the class starts?

    a. Is, know
    b. Do, knows
    c. Does, know
    d. Does, knows

____3. Are you going to see your friend tomorrow?
    No, _____ to.

    a. I'm not go
    b. I not going
    c. I won't go
    d. I'm not going

____4. Where do you wait for your friend? _____ the corner.

    a. By
    b. In
    c. On
    d. To

____5. Hiromi _____ much last night.

    a. wasn't study
    b. wasn't studying
    c. hasn't studying
    d. didn't studies

____6. Our relatives just heard a concert. _____ soloist was outstanding.

    a. A
    b. An
    c. The
    d. No word needed

____7. She saw _____ people on the street yesterday.

    a. many
    b. much
    c. a lot
    d. a little

____8. Jane's sister _____ dinner all week.

    a. cook
    b. has cooked
    c. has cooking
    d. has been cooked

____9. Where are you going to be this Saturday? _____ to be at home.

  a. I'll
  b. I go
  c. I going
  d. I'm going

____10. Bob's roommate asked him to go to Arizona with him, but Bob said no. When Bob met Bill later that day, he said:

  a. I was able to go to Arizona with my roomette.
  b. I could go to Arizona with my roommate.
  c. I should have gone to Arizona with my roommate
  d. I could have gone to Arizona with my roommate.

____11. Chang was in Tokyo in 1964. He went to the Olympics. Today he tells a friend:

  a. I could go to the Olympics in Tokyo.
  b. I could have gone to the Olympics in Tokyo.
  c. I was able to go to the Olympics in Tokyo.
  d. I may have gone to the Olympics in Tokyo.

____12. Jane is going to meet Betty at the concert tonight. The doors will be closed exactly at 8:15, and no one is admitted after the doors are closed. Betty tells Jane to be on time. She says:

  a. We don't need to be late.
  b. We musn't be late.
  c. We don't have to be late.
  d. We may not be late.

_____13. It is Saturday morning. At six o'clock, Tom's alarm
       clock goes off. Tom starts to get up. His roommate says:

   a. It's Saturday; you musn't get up.
   b. It's Saturday; you don't have to get up.
   c. It's Saturday; you could not get up.
   d. It's Saturday; you should not get up.

_____14. Betty's little sister has the measles. She scratches her
       arms constantly. Betty told her not to scratch, but she said:

   a. I must .
   b. I would rather.
   c. I can't help it (without thinking about it).
   d. I ought to.

_____15. Doris/ notebook = possession

   a. Doris' notebook.
   b. Doris's notebook.
   c. the notebook of Doris.
   d. Dorises' notebook.

PART TWO: WORD ORDER

_____16. eyes/girl/who works in my office/blue = possession

   a. the girl's eyes who works in my office are blue.
   b. the girls' eyes who works in my office are blue.
   c. the eyes of the girl who works in my office are blue.
   d. the girlz' eyes are blue who works in my office.

_____17. The Harrises/house

   a. the house of the Harris'
   b. the Harris' house
   c. the Harrises' house
   d. the Harrises'es house

_____18. New York/big/Chicago = compare

    a. New York is bigger than Chicago.
    b. New York is bigger than Illinois.
    c. New York is biger than Chicago.
    d. New York is more big than Chicago.

_____19. Harry speaks French well/than he speaks Spanish = compare

    a. Harry speaks French weller than he speaks Spanish.
    b. Harry speaks French best than he speaks Spanish.
    c. Harry speaks French gooder than he speaks Spanish.
    d. Harry speaks French better than he speaks Spanish.

_____20. Which is the correct word order?

    a. I'm going to let George to do it.
    b. I'm going to let George do it.
    c. I'm going to let it to do George.
    d. I'm going to George do it.

_____21. Indicate the correct word order.

    a. Do you want me to go?
    b. Do you want that I go?
    c. Do you want to go me?
    d. Do you want I to go?

_____22. Our teacher

    a. reads aloud often in class.
    b. often reads aloud in class.
    c. in class reads aloud often.
    d. aloud often reads in class.

_____23. Do you want

    a. with me to go to a party tonight?
    b. tonight to a party to go with me?
    c. to go to a party with me tonight?
    d. to go with me to a party tonight?

_____24. Joe Harris has

    a. his Spanish class here in the morning.
    b. here his Spanish class in the morning
    c. in the morning here his Spanish class.
    d. Spanish his class in the morning here.

_____25. I like (referring to something in general).

    a. very much the coffee.
    b. the coffee very much
    c. coffee very much

_____26. Did John

    a. finish his homework before supper?
    b. finished his homework before supper?
    c. he finish his homework before supper?
    d. finish her homework before supper?

_____27. Indicate the correct word order.

    a. I an studying at the Institute since 2 years ago.
    b. Since 2 years ago I study at the Institute.
    c. I have been studying at the Institute for 2 years.
    d. I have been studying the Institute for 2 years.

_____28. Did you have time to _____ good-bye when he leaves
    home?
      a. say   b. tell

____29. My father always _____ me good-bye when he leaves home.

a. say
b. says
c. tells
d. tell

____30. Jane: "I'll go to Boston in January." Jane said she _____ to Boston in January.

a. will go
b. shall go
c. would go
d. went

____31. Jane to Betty: "You should write to your grandmother." Jane told Betty that she _____ to her grandmother.

a. should write
b. could write
c. could have written
d. should have written

____32. Indicate the correct word order.

a. You should never cross the street when cars approach.
b. You should never crossing the street when cars approach.
c. You should never to go across the street when cars approach.
d. You should never to cross the street when cars approach.

____33. Joe to Pete: "You would get better grades if you studied harder. "You _____ better grades if you'd studied last semester."

a. would get
b. would got
c. would have gotten
d. would have getten

_____34. Harry: "Okay, Ted, we have the flowers. I will give Mr. Jones the money."

    a. Harry paid for the flowers.
    b. Harry paid to the flowers.
    c. Harry paid the flowers.
    d. Harry paid back the flowers.

_____35. The airplane left the airport at 5:30.

    a. The airplane took off.
    b. The airplane took up.
    c. The airplane took in.
    d. The airplane took down.

PART THREE: READING COMPREHENSION

Directions: Read each passage carefully. Then answer the questions by indicating a., b., c., or d. on the line on the left margin.

_____1. It takes a lot of money for a person to begin a new business.

    a. People take a lot of money from a new person with a new business.
    b. Starting a new business requires much money.
    c. People with a new business get lots of money.
    d. New businesses take in lots of money.

_____2. Bill: "Pablo, you should've gone to the movies with me last night. You would've had a good time."

    a. Pablo went to the movies with Bill.
    b. Pablo went to the movies with Betty.
    c. Pablo didn't go to the movies with Bill.
    d. Pablo didn't go to the movies with Betty.

3. For many years, until 1926, movies were silent. They had neither sound nor music to go with them. The actors only made motions, while the words they spoke were printed on the screen. In the theater a musician played the piano or organ, while the film was shown. Many movie stars came to fame in the silent days -- Mary Pickford with her beautiful curls, William S. Hart in cowboy films, such comedians as Harold Lloyd and the great Charlie Chaplin. Many films were serials, which told a long story that had a new chapter every week.

____A. The early movies

    a. had sound.
    b. had music.
    c. had sound and music.
    d. had neither sound nor music.

____B. In the early movie theaters

    a. people only watched the screen and heard no music.
    b. people heard jazz.
    c. people heard a musician playing the piano.
    d. people heard a musician playing the drums.

____C. William S. Hart was a popular
    a. comedian.
    b. director.
    c. villain.
    d. cowboy.

4. In the development of literature, prose generally comes late. Verse is more effective for oral delivery and more easily retained in the memory. It is, therefore, a rather remarkable fact that English possessed a considerable body of prose literature in the ninth century, at a time when most other modern languages in Europe had barely developed a literature in verse. This unusual accomplishment was due to the inspiration of one man, King Alfred the Great, who ruled from 871 to 899. When he ascended the throne, Alfred found that learning, which in the previous century had placed England in the forefront of

Europe, had greatly declined. In an effort to restore his country to something like its former state, he undertook to provide for his people certain books in English; books which he deemed most essential to their welfare. In preparation for this task, he set about in mature life to learn Latin.

_____A. According to the information given in the paragraph, King Alfred may most properly be regarded as the father of English

    a. poetry.
    b. learning.
    c. prose.
    d. literature.

_____B. The writer suggests that the earliest English poetry was

    a. written in very difficult language.
    b. not intended to be read silently.
    c. never really popular with the public.
    d. less original than later poetry.

_____C. According to the paragraph, England's learning had brought it to the "forefront of Europe" in the
    a. seventh century.
    b. eighth century.
    c. ninth century.
    d. tenth century.

_____D. The writer suggests that at the time of King Alfred most of the other modern languages of Europe had

    a. both a verse and a prose literature.
    b. a literature in prose but not in verse.
    c. neither a prose nor a verse literature.
    d. a literature in verse but not in prose.

____E. We may conclude from the paragraph that the books which Alfred "deemed most essential" were

a. already available in another language.
b. written largely in verse.
c. later translated into Latin.
d. original with Alfred himself.

PART FOUR: MECHANICS

Directions: Decide what punctuation should be used in the numbered spaces. Write the letter of your choice in the space provided at the left of each number. Example: A red$_0$ blue$_1$ and pink car.

____0.
> The correct answer is "b," a comma.

a. .
b. ,
c. :
d. ;

At 9$_1$30 A M$_2$ on columbus$_3$ Day$_4$ which is not a school holiday$_5$ a fire broke out in the chemistry building of emerson high school.$_6$ professor montague$_7$ left his office at this moment$_8$ He said$_9$ $_{10}$wow$_{11}$ what a sight$_{12}$

____1.   ____2.   ____3.   ____4.

a. ;   a. AM.   a. columbus   a. .
b. :   b. A.M   b. columbuS   b. ,
c. .   .   c. A.M.   c. Columbus   c. ;
d. ,   d. A,M,   d. ColumbuS   d. :

____5.   ____6.

a. ;   a. Emerson high school
b. :   b. emerson High School
c. .   c. Emerson High school
d. ,   d. Emerson High School

____7.   ____8.

a. professor montague   a. :
b. Professor Montague   b. ,
c. professor Montague   c. ?
d. Professor montague   d. .

____9.   ____10.   ____11.   ____12.

a. ,   a. "wow   a. ,   a. .
b. :   b. "Wow   b. :   b. ."
c. ?   c. Wow   c. ;   c. :"
d. ;   d. wow   d. !   d. !"

Returning to his friend Peter$_1$ Bill asked$_2$ whether he still wished to continue with the trip$_3$

____1.   ____2.   ____3.

a. :   a. ;   a. ?
b. ;   b. ,"   b. ?"
c. ,   c. ;"   c. .
d. .   d. no punctuation   d. "

END OF INTERMEDIATE PLACEMENT EVALUATION

ADVANCED EVALUATION

PART ONE: DISCRIMINATION

Write the word (a., b., c., or d.) which best completes the sentences on the line provided.

1. _____ham costs eighty cents a pound.
   a. an   b. the   c. big   d. ____.

2. Where is _____Red Sea located?
   a. a   b. the   c. at   d. ____.

3. Mr. Naga works for _____telephone company.
   a. the   b. a   c. one   d. it

4. _____Mexicans are friendly.
   a. the   b. a   c. much   d. ____.

5. I'd like _____toast.
   a. a   b. a piece of   c. a bar of   d. ____.

6. She lives in _____United States.
   a. a   b. same   c. the   d. ____.

7. I'm taking _____ history.
   a. the   b. some   c. an   d. ____.

8. Is this sentence correct in English?
   John is wanting a cup of coffee?
   a. yes.   b. no.

9. He gives me a book. Yesterday he _____.
   a. is giving   b. gaved   c. gave d. give

10. The performance begins immediately. Last night it _____.
   a. begin   b. began   c. begun   d. beganed

11. The flag is still flying. Question (?) _____.
   a. Is the flag still flying?   c. Does the flag flying?
   b. The flag is still flying?   d. Does is the flag fly?

12. The man writes a song. Past, question (?) _____.
   a. Does the man write a song? c. Did the man
                                      write a song?
   b. Did the man wrote a song? d. Wrote the man a song?

13. The firing stops. past, question (?) _____.
   a. Did the fire stop?   c. Did the firing
                                       stopped?
   b. Stopped the firing?   d.Did the firing stop?

14. I'm going to let her _____.
   a. go   b. to go   c. going   d. want

15. I want her _____.
   a. to go   b. go   c. goed   d. to went

16. I want:
   a. an advice b. 1 advice c. a bit of advice d. advice

17. Helen wants (2) (furniture) _____.
   a. two furnitures   c. two bits of furniture
   b. two pieces of furniture   d. two sticks of furniture

18. I bought the book _____ them.
   a. to   b. from   c. at   d. By

19. Mr. Naga translated the document _____ me.
   a. to   b. for   c. in   d. on

20. Mr. and Mrs. Harris/house _____.
   a. Mr. and Mrs. Harris house   c. Mr. and Mrs. Harri's house
   b. Mr. and Firs. Barris' house   d. the house of Mr. and Mrs.
      Harris

21. Our family doctor smokes (present perfect) a pipe for a long
    time. _____.
    a. has smoked b. has spoken c. have smoked d. have spoken

22. Does your sister speak French (present perfect) for a long
    time? _____.
    a. has spoken your sister   c. has speaked your sister
    b. has your sister spoken   d. has spoked your sister

23. Whose pronunciation is the _____ in the class?
    a. better   b. bitter   c. more good   d. best

24. Mr. Carson is the _____ in the class.
    a. taller   b. most tall   c. tallest   d. more tall

25. Jane drives _____ of her three sisters.
    a. very carefully   c. more carefully
    b. the most carefully   d. the carefullest

26. The orchestra (direct) by Toscanini last night._____.
    a. was direct   b. will be directed   c. were directed
    d. was directed

27. A new apartment house (build) on my street now. _____.
    a. is build.   b. is being   c. was built   d. has
                        built   been built

28. How many languages (speak) in Switzerland? _____.
    a. is spoken b. was spoken c. are spoken d. are speaked

29. John, _____ , is a Boy Scout.
    a. who eats hamburgers   c. where eats hamburgers
    b. which eats hamburgers   d. eats hamburgers

30. Paris, _____ , is lovely.
    a. which is the capital of France
    b. where is the capital of France
    c. that is the capital of France
    d. who is the capital of France

PART TWO: MECHANICS

Using the past modal indicated, change each of the following sentences.
Example: By tomorrow, we finish this course. (FUTURE)
=>   By tomorrow, we will have finished this course.

1. We stay at the performance past 11:00 P.M. (ADVISABILITY)
2. Pablo and Yukio study hard to get 100% on every test. (INFERENCE)
3. Alicia leaves her house early. (POSSIBILITY)
4. Harry gets to bed early for a change. (NECESSITY)
5. The effects of good government are felt far into the future. (CONDITION)

If necessary, correct each of the following conditional sentences. Explain the meaning of your new sentence.

Example: If I had time, I'd help you.
=> If I have time, I'll help you. (a possible situation - I hope so.)
OR If I had time, I'd help you. (an unlikely situation - I'm sorry.)

1. Luis would have found his girlfriend if he waited a little longer.
2. If we'd known each other longer, we'd have more in common.
3. If the rain continues, we'll have to get under cover.
4. Mike likes to drive around a lot if he has a new car to show off.
5. The pharmacist could fill your prescription if you tell him what you need.

Using a relative pronoun ("who," "which," "that," or "whose"), combine the following pairs of sentences. Watch punctuation. List the subject and verb of each sentence.

> Example: I met a man. He came from France.
> =>   I met a man who came from France.
>   S = "I"; V = "met"; RS = "man"; RV = "came"

1. I bought the books yesterday. One of the books is used.
2. Luis is always asking questions. He will learn quickly.
3. Food Market business is increasing. Food Market hopes to add new stores next year.
4. The tree was in our front yard. The tree blocked a lot of light.
5. The fly was inside the clock. The fly flew out of the clock when it struck one.

Using a participle, combine each of the following pairs of sentences. Underline the participle and tell which word it describes.

> Example: John drove down the street. John hit a pole.
> => Driving down the street, John hit a pole. ("driving" describes "John.")

1. Hiromi slept until 10:00. She got to work and was fired.
2. Antonio was raised in the country. He went only to one-room schools.
3. "Faust" was written by a German. It was popular all over the world.
4. The fighter got a black eye. He couldn't see for a week.
5. We headed out of town. We got a flat tire.

PART THREE: COMPOSITION

Describe an interesting person. It may be a member of your family: one of your parents or grandparents, a brother, sister, cousin, aunt or uncle. It may be a friend or a person you know. Be specific in describing the special characteristics that you think make him or her an interesting person. You may wish to give examples of things this person has said or done which illustrate these characteristics.

END OF ADVANCED PLACEMENT EVALUATION

EVALUATION FOR READING COMPREHENSION

Part One:

The sentences below are taken from the Trinity University catalogue. Read carefully and answer the questions that follow.

GENERAL INFORMATION

The University is a corporate member of the American Association of University Women, and its women graduates are eligible for membership in this organization.

COMPLIANCE POLICY

Within published requirements for admission, Trinity University does not and will not discriminate in admission of students to study at the University, enrollment in classes, housing or use of facilities in the academic program because of race, color, religion, sex, age, marital status, national origin, disability, veteran or disabled veteran status.

The University takes affirmative action to ensure that applicants are employed, and that employees are treated during employment, without regard to their race, color, religion, sex, age, marital status, national origin, disability, veteran or disabled veteran status. Such action includes, but is not limited to, employment, upgrading, demotion or transfer, recruitment or recruitment advertising, layoff or termination, rates of pay or other forms of compensation, and selection for employment training, including apprenticeship.

Vocabulary words:

affirmative—agreeable
apprentice—beginner
compensation—pay
compliance—following rules
corporate—united
demote—made lower
discriminate—show prejudice
eligible—qualified
employ—give work
enrollment—registration
ensure—make sure
facility—place

graduate—completed degree
include—take in
layoff—put out of work
limit—maximum amount
marital—married
membership—part of
rate—amount
regard—attention
requirement—need
select—chose
status—state
treat—deal with

In the following statements, choose the correct answer, a, b, c, or d needed to complete the statement:

1. The general information tells us about_____.
   a. Association b. corporate member c. America d. organization

2. Compliance policy is_____.
   a. about requirement b. a set of rules c. a plan of study
   d. an academic program

3. The American Association of University Women accepts
_____.
   a. every woman b. women with good grades c. teachers only
   d. women graduates

4. There is no information about _____.
   a. grades b. the TOEFL test c. affirmative action d. marriage

5. If you want to know about the compliance policy, _____.
   a. ask a teacher b. ask a policeman
   c. read general information d. ask a student

6. Persons may not be discriminated on the basis of _____.
   a. good grades b. good looks c. color d. their parents

7. The University takes affirmative action _____.
   a. to ensure salaries b. to ensure employment of all applicants
   c. to lay off employees d. to hire women

8. All employees and students are treated _____.
   a. fairly b. according to sex c. regarding color d. by age

9. Affirmative action includes _____.
   a. good behavior b. good grades c. employment d. all courses

10. Everyone is protected by _____.
    a. apprenticeship b. affirmative action c. marriage
    d. student parking

Part Two:

The following is a news article. Read carefully, then respond to the questions below.

Illnesses Rising in Hurricane's Aftermath

TEGUCIGALPA, Honduras, Nov. 15 (Agence France-Presse) - Young children are falling victim to infections after last month's hurricane, the Honduran Health Minister, Marco Rosa, said today.

Large areas of stagnant water left by the floods are breeding grounds for malaria-carrying mosquitoes, he said. In the slums around Tegucigalpa, 50,000 children have been exposed to malaria and many more are threatened across the country.

Similar fears were spreading throughout Central America. Today Nicaragua began an extensive campaign to vaccinate more than a million children and their mothers. Nicaragua also reported 31,888 cases of acute respiratory infections, 422 cases of diarrhea and 150 cases of cholera; Honduras recorded 858 cases of malaria, 53,617 cases of respiratory illnesses, 12,393 cases of gastrointestinal ailments and 2 cases of cholera.

In Guatemala at least eight people have died of cholera since Thursday.

Vocabulary words:

across—everywhere	gastrointestinal—stomach
acute—serious, severe	infected—diseased
aftermath—a result	report—tell, inform
area—place	respiratory—breathing
around—near, here and there	similar—almost the same
breed—reproduce	slums—poor housing
campaign—battle, effort	spread—extend itself
expose—leave unprotected	stagnant—foul, dirty
extensive—far reaching	threaten—put to danger
fall victim—become sick	throughout—everywhere
fear—be afraid	vaccinate—inoculate

For the 10 statements below choose a,b,c, or d, whichever completes the statement correctly:

1. Young children are falling victim to _____.
   a. breeding grounds   b. infections   c. fears   d. water

2. According to the news _____ have been exposed.
   a 3,000 children   b. 50,000 children   c. 5,000 children
   d. 40,000 children

3. Large areas _____.
   a. had no water   b. had stagnant water   c. had mosquitoes
   d. were breeding grounds

4. Most persons threatened were _____.
   a. children   b. grownups   c. teachers   d. students

5. Many more children were threatened _____.
   a. in Central America   b. across the country   c. in the slums
   d. by weather

6. Nicaragua began _____.
   a. a campaign to vaccinate   b. an infection
   c. vaccination of mothers   d. cleanup

7. Fears were spreading _____.
   a. across Central America   b. during the campaign
   c. during vaccination   d. around the country

8. In Nicaragua there were 150 cases of _____.
   a. malaria   b. cholera   c. respiratory illness   d. infections

9. Honduras recorded 858 cases of _____.
   a. cholera   b. infections   c. malaria   d. respiratory illness

10. Guatemala recorded 8 _____.
    a. deaths   b. campaigns   c. ailments   d. fears

Part Three:

The following article is a news report by the Associated Press. Study carefully, then choose the correct responses.

Two earthquakes jolt rural region in China

ASSOCIATED PRESS

BEIJING — Two earthquakes struck a rural area in southwestern China, killing one person and destroying scores of homes, Chinese seismologists said Friday.

Hundreds of people were seriously injured.

A magnitude-5 quake struck the Ninglang Yi Autonomous County in Yunnan province and neighboring Yanyuan County in Sichuan province Thursday. A 6.2 quake shook the area minutes later.

The quakes injured 1,383 people, 210 of them seriously, the Central Seismology Bureau reported. Many were injured from houses collapsing, said a bureau spokesman who gave only his surname, Wu.

The quakes destroyed the houses of 230 families and three schools, and a landslide blocked a river, the state-run Xinhua News Agency reported.

Losses were estimated at $24 million, Xinhua said, and clothing, food and medicine are being sent to the area.

Quakes measuring 5.3 and 5.2 hit the same area, about 1,200 miles southwest of Beijing, in October.

A magnitude-5 quake can cause considerable damage, while a magnitude-6 tremor, 10 times as severe, can result in severe damage.

Vocabulary words:

block—stop
collapse—fall apart
considerable—great, large
damage—loss, injury
destroy—demolish
earthquake—tremor
estimate—calculate
jolt—shake
landslide—moving earth
loss—ruin
magnitude—extent

measure—size
neighboring—next to
region—area
rural—country
scores—many
seismologist—quake scientist
serious—important
severe—serious
strike—hit
shake—quake, jolt
surname—family name

For the 10 statements below, choose a,b,c, or d, whichever correctly completes the statement:

1. Earthquakes in a rural area of China destroyed _____.
   a. scores of homes   b. one policeman   c. many children
   d. some teachers

2. _____of people were seriously injured.
   a. Thousands   b. Hundreds   c. Millions   d. Dozens

3. The first quake was a _____.
   a. magnitude-2   b. magnitude-4   c. magnitude-7   d. magnitude-5

4. The earthquake struck on _____.
   a. Monday   b. Friday   c. Sunday   d. Thursday

5. The quakes injured _____people seriously.
   a. 7   b. 324   c. 1,280   d. 210

6. Many were injured when _____.
   a. lightning struck   b. streets were destroyed   c. it rained
   d. houses collapsed

7. The spokesman was someone with_____.
   a. curiosity   b. a nice car   c. magnitude   d. the surname Wu

8. The quake destroyed the houses of _____.
   a. 20 families   b. 350 families   c. 670 families   d. 230 families

9. Losses were estimated at_____.
   a. little value   b. no value   c. small importance   d. $24 million

10. A magnitude-6 quake is _____as severe as a magnitude-5 tremor.
    a. 5 times   b. 7 times   c. 3 times   d. ten times

Part Four:

The following text is part of Trinity University's instructions for continuing and undergraduate students. Read carefully to find the correct responses.

REGISTRATION INSTRUCTIONS
UNDERGRADUATE STUDENTS
CONTINUING STUDENTS

Undergraduate students enrolled for the Fall Semester, register for the Spring Semester during the registration period, November 9-20. After meeting with your faculty advisor, bring a signed *STUDENT SCHEDULE PLANNING FORM* to the Office of the Registrar (Northrup Hall, Room 113) during or after the time period for your last name shown on the Registration Schedule.

NOTE WELL:

(1) All students must clear any balances due the University with the Business Office prior to registering for classes.

(2) Continuing students registering after November 20 will be assessed the $100.00 late registration fee.

Bills for the Spring Semester will be mailed to students at the home address (unless other arrangements are made in advance with the Business Office) after registration with payment due by December 31. Students who have not paid their spring charges or made appropriate arrangements in writing with the Business Office by December 31, will be assessed a $100.00 late fee or will have their registrations canceled. Students who are canceled must register during LATE REGISTRATION on January 11, the following year, and will be assessed the $100.00 late fee.

NEW AND READMITTED STUDENTS

New and readmitted undergraduate students will register for the Spring Semester on Monday, January 11, from 8:30 a.m. to 11:30 a.m. A completed *STUDENT SCHEDULE PLANNING FORM* signed by the faculty advisor must be presented at the Office of the Registrar in Northrup Hall, Room 113 to register. Registration is then completed by paying all charges at the Business Office no later than January 11. Late registration during Add/Drop will be assessed the $100.00 Late Registration

Vocabulary words:

advance—ahead
advisor—counselor
appropriate—special
arrangement—special way
assess—evaluate, fine
balance—what remains
canceled—terminated
charge—fee, payment

clear—take care
completed—fixed, done
continue—go on
enroll—register
fee—payment, charge
following—next
period—time
prior—before

Complete the following statements with the choices given in a, b, c, or d, after careful consideration:

1. Undergraduate students must register during the month of
_____ for the coming Spring semester.
a. September b. March c. January d. November

2. Students should enroll during the _____period.
a. vacation b. recess c. registration d. study

3. Students register as their _____ _____are shown.
a. last names b. bad grades c. first names d. dues

4. If your name is Perez, you may register before _____.
a. Angellini b. Saroyan c. Bishop d. Lozano

5. All students must clear any_____due.
a. snow b. balances c. books d. homework

6. If you register after November, you'll have to pay _____.
a. some money b. late registration fee c. $200 d) $300

7. Bills will be mailed to the _____address.
a. old b. new c. home d. business

8. New students will register for the Spring Semester in_____.
a. January b. February c. March d. June

9. Student Planning Schedule Form must be signed by _____.
a. your parents   b. the dean   c. faculty advisor   d. student

10) Registration is completed by paying _____.
a. some charges   b. selected charges   c. later   d. all charges

Part Five:

The following is a news article. Read carefully and fill in the right expression where necessary.

Lava starts to flow at Mexico volcano
ASSOCIATED PRESS

COLIMA, Mexico - Lava began to surge up Friday in the crater of the rumbling Colima Volcano, leading experts to predict the smoking peak would stage a "low-intensity" emission of molten rock rather than the explosive eruption some had feared.

The appearance of the lava, detected during a helicopter flight by researchers over the 12,700-foot peak, forced authorities in southern Colima state to put off plans to let residents of an evacuated village return to their homes.

"The developments indicate that a low intensity lava flow has begun...if it continues, it would overflow onto one of the volcano's slopes," the state government said in a statement.

All 140 village residents were evacuated Wednesday from Yerba Buena after the volcano gave signals of an impending eruption stronger than any seen in decades.

The volcano exploded in 1913, shattering windows and showering ash in towns several miles away.

Vocabulary words:

crater—mouth of volcano
decade—ten years
detect—discover
emission—discharge
eruption—bursting forth
evacuate—remove
expert—experienced person
impending—threatening
indicate—show, point out
intensity—force, energy
lava—melted volcano rock

molten—melted
peak—mountain top
predict—foretell
put off—postpone
rumble—rolling sound
several—a few
shatter—destroy
slope—fall, rise
stage—create
surge—stream, come out of

Below are ten incomplete statements. Choose the correct expression, a., b., c., or d., to complete them.

1. _____ surged up in the crater of the volcano.
a. Sound b. Fire c. Lava d. Experts

2. It led _____ to predict a "low intensity" emission.
a. people b. experts c. spectators d. visitors

3. The volcano staged an _____of _____ _____.
a. emission; molten rock b. explosive eruption; lava
   c. unexpected flow; fire d. awesome surge; heat

4. The lava was detected during a _____ _____.
a. helicopter flight b. nice morning c. late evening
   d. loud noise

5. Residents of an evacuated village were ____ able to return to their homes.
a. almost b. surely c. not d. clearly

6. The developments indicated that low _____lava flow has begun.
a. emission b. intensity c. surge d. predicted

7. The population of the village was _____ residents.
a. 21,000 b. 473 c. 140 d. 410

8. All of the village residents were _____.
a. happy b. evacuated c. dead d. strong

9. The volcano gave signals of an _____eruption.
a. impending b. ongoing c. explosive d. intense

10. When the volcano erupted in 1913, it _____windows in towns
a few miles away.
a. forced b. shattered c. showered d. evacuated

PROGRESS EVALUATION

Let's Begin
(Chapter 3)

1. Listen and Write

   a._____

   b._____

   c._____

   d._____

   e._____

2. Change the following statements to yes/no questions.

Example: Pedro and Alice are talking.
<u>Are Pedro and Alice talking</u>?

a. Hiromi and José are studying. _____

b. Manuel and Angel are eating. _____

c. Victoria and Isaac are coming. _____

d. Hiromi and José are happy. _____

e. Mr. and Mrs. Naga are sad. _____

f. The Carsons are hungry. _____

Example: The bus is late.
<u>Is the bus late</u>?

a. Ann is on time. _____

b. Louis is late. _____

c. Ann is early. _____

d. Angel is never late. _____

e. Manuel is sometimes on time. _____

3. <u>What</u> questions.

Example: My name is Pedro
                <u>What's your name</u>?

a. His name is Manuel.   _____
b. It's time to get up.   _____
c. Her brother's name is Yukio.   _____
d. Their sister's name is Michiyo._____
e. Our telephone number is 436-0152. _____

4. Change the following commands to polite request.

Example: Close the door.   (would, please)
                <u>Would you, please, close the door</u>.

a. Come to my office. (would, please)

_____

b. Read the lesson. (shall, now)

_____

c. Come in. (please)

_____

d. Eat your dinner. (would, please)

_____

e. Practice the dialogue. (let's)

_____

PROGRESS EVALUATION

Let's Converse
(Chapter 3)

1. Dictation (Word Spelling)

a._____. f._____.
b._____. g._____.
c._____. h._____.
d._____. i._____.
e._____. j._____.

2. Make new sentences with the words in parentheses.

a. Let's go to the <u>bookstore</u>. (supermarket)

_____.

b. We're studying <u>chapter</u> <u>three</u>. (math)

_____.

c. You're buying <u>school</u> <u>supplies</u>. (apples)

_____.

d. They're for <u>my</u> <u>friend</u>. (Carol)

_____.

e. <u>She</u> can show you around. (Pamela)

_____.

f. That's a good <u>idea</u>. (book)

_____.

g. <u>We</u> get them mixed up. (They)

_____.

h. <u>I</u> can think of it. (David)

_____.

i. They're easy to <u>lose</u>. (remember)

_____.

j. It's <u>my</u> weak subject. (her)

_____.

3. In Column II, answer the question using the word in paretheses.

COLUMN II

a. What's this? (book)   _____.
b. What's this? (pencil)   _____.
c. What's this? (eraser)   _____.
d. What's this? (envelope)   _____.
e. What's this? (coin)   _____.
f. What are these? (books)   _____.
g. What are these? (pencils)   _____.
h. What are these? (erasers)   _____.
i. What are these? (envelopes) _____.
j. What are these? (coins)   _____.

4. Supply negative response.

a. Do you need a book?   _____.
b. Does she need supplies?   _____.
c. Do they need notebooks?   _____.
d. Does Carol need a pencil?   _____.
e. Does David need love?   _____.

5. Give the meaning for the following IDIOMS.

a. I'm an *easy-going* man.   _____.
b. Tom is in *the know*.   _____.
c. This is neither *here* nor *there*. _____.

PROGRESS EVALUATION

Let's Read
(Chapter 4)

A. Substitute where possible, the synonym of the underlined word, or a phrase that explains the meaning. Make other necessary changes.

Example: His _conduct_ changed.

His behavior was different.

1. You won't hear any <u>noise</u>. _____.
2. You'll say it <u>forcefully</u>. _____.
3. We should be able to <u>accomplish</u> a common goal.

_____.
4. I am aware of my <u>duties</u>. _____.
5. I <u>pledge</u> this to you. _____.
6. He <u>delivered</u> a fine speech. _____.
7. It was <u>hard</u> to lose. _____.
8. The students voted for their <u>favorite</u> candidate.

_____.
9. Some day I'll work to <u>change</u> that. _____.
10. We will proceed with <u>care</u>. _____.

B. In the space on the left write the word(s) that best fit the underlined expression. Make other necessary changes.

1. _____. Mrs. Campbell sensed something unsual in her son's <u>conduct</u>.
2. _____. They <u>elected</u> me.
3. _____. I'm <u>pleased</u> they want you.
4. _____. You haven't eaten your <u>evening meal</u>.
5. _____. This is <u>pressing</u>.
6. _____. His parents <u>warned</u> him.

105

7. _____.   Mike asked his father <u>abruptly</u>.
8. _____.   Mrs. Campbell knew how to <u>support</u>
                             Mike.
9. _____.   It is our <u>obligation</u> to communicate.
10. _____.   The <u>reply</u> will be also <u>sensible</u>.

C. Write T for True in front of each statement that you think is
   true. Write F for False if the statement is not true.

_____ 1. Mike was always excited.
_____ 2. He spoke calmly to his mother.
_____ 3. Mrs. Campbell suggested a cola.
_____ 4. Miss Campbell cautioned her son.
_____ 5. Mike went to sleep late.
_____ 6. He always ate supper with the family.
_____ 7. Mike's dressing habits changed.
_____ 8. The Campbells listened to Mike's speech.
_____ 9. It was easy for Mike to prepare his speech.
_____ 10. He promised to change the system.

D. In Column I are the beginnings of sentences. In Column II
   are the completions to sentences of Column I. Select the
   completion best fitting each sentence in Column I according
   to the narrative.

<u>Column I</u>   <u>Column II</u>

1. Mike has never been   a. as the Campbells had wished.
2. He came home from school   b. this way all the time.
3. They sat   c. on a merry-go-round.
4. I think they had   d. a good speech.
5. Mike was constantly   e. earlier than usual.
6. I would slow down   f. at the table.
7. I will rest   g. if I could.
8. If only he would dress   h. this excited before.
9. A complete change   i. for Mike to prepare his speech.
10. I'll impress people   j. tomorrow to listen.
11. I'll prepare   k. as a neat dresser.
12. Mrs. Campbell knew   l. when it's all over.

13. It hadn't been easy
14. I'll be at school
15. We have a
16. It was not

m. how to encourage Mike.
n. a wide choice of candidates.
o. came over Mike's dressing habits.
p. good school here.

PROGRESS EVALUATION

Let's Write
(Chapter 4-5)

A. Make any necessary changes when you substitute the new element into your sentence:

1. Love means different things to different <u>people</u>. (men)

   _____.

2. <u>Children</u> regard love from <u>their</u> point of view. (we)

   _____.

3. As <u>we</u> grow older, love changes. (they)

   _____.

4. Love changes constantly because <u>we</u> change. (you)

   _____.

5. Family love means being <u>your</u> natural self. (my)

   _____.

6. Before thinking of <u>themselves,</u> <u>parents</u> will help <u>their</u> children. (myself, I, my)

   _____.

7. As long as <u>man</u> <u>has</u> existed, family love has been the corner stone of civilized society. (we)

   _____.

8. <u>You</u> <u>feel</u> a lasting affection. (she)

   _____.

9. <u>You</u> search out one another. (we)

   _____.

10. <u>Two</u> <u>people</u> unite into one. (they)

    _____.

11. <u>You</u> want to give everything to <u>the</u> <u>person</u> <u>you</u> <u>love</u>. (I, her)

    _____.

12. <u>You're</u> <u>not</u> afraid of death. (one is)

    _____.

B. Supply the missing subordinators (clause markers) for each blank space.

Example: _Although_ much has been written about love, we love.

1. _____ we are puzzled, we ask "what is love?"
2. Some regard love from one point of view, _____ they are very young.
3. _____ we grow older, love grows with us.
4. _____ true love comes, you feel happy.
5. You feel a lasting affection for each other, _____ you search out one another.
6. _____ you've found love, you're no longer afraid.
7. Sick persons can become well again, _____ love enters their hearts.
8. Love brings people together, _____ they care.

C. In the spaces provided below, write your own complex sentences. Follow the directions given before each group.

a. Use a comma (,) and the subordinator "although."

1.) _____.
2.) _____.

b. Use a comma (,) and the subordinator "after."

1.) _____.
2.) _____.

c. Use a colon (:) and a direct quotation

1.) _____.
2.) _____.

D. Fill in each blank space provided in the sentences below
with the list of words and phrases.

live; is called; are; is; reading; learn; died; has; go; moving;
attends; to study; does; loves; read; to read; studying

    The street on which the Axbys now _____ is called Shadywood.
It _____ Shadywood because there _____ many shade trees
there. Prior to _____ there, the Axbys _____on
Blanco Street. Mr. Axby _____ a school teacher and a widower.
Mrs. Axby _____ during the past summer after a long illness.
Mr. Axby _____ three children _____ who still
of school age. The siblings _____ to neighborhood schools.
Ralph _____ _____ is the oldest and the tallest at the age
of seventeen. He _____ Meridian High School and _____ well
in school. John _____ _____ and _____ _____.
Their sister Dorothy _____ of _____ rapidly but unable
well.

E. Supply the missing prepositions for each blank space.

1. The street _____ which the Axbys now live is called
Shadywood.
2. Prior _____ moving there, the Axbys lived _____ Blanco
      Street.
3. Mrs. Axby died _____ a long illness.
4. Three children are _____ school age.
5. The siblings go _____ neighborhood schools.
6. He is the tallest _____ the age of seventeen.
7. John is a freshman _____ the same school.
8. He loves _____ study and _____ read.
9. Their sister is _____ the eighth grade.

F. Write the appropriate present tense form of the verb in
parentheses.

1. The street on which Ralph _____ (to live) is called
    Shadywood.

2. It _____ (to be called) Shadywood because there _____ (to be) many shade trees there.
3. Mr. Axby _____ (to have) three children who _____ (to be) still of school age.
4. Ralph _____ (to have) a brother and a sister.
5. He _____ (to attend) Meridian High School and _____ (to play) tennis on the team.

G. Select the word (or phrase) from the following list that best completes each of the sentences below. You may use one selection more than once.

nearby; quick; is busy; purchase; to leave; rainy weather; dead; called; parking; place; illness

1. The <u>name</u> of the street is Shadywood. It is _____ Shadywood Street.
2. Mrs. Axby <u>died</u> after a long illness. She has been _____ since the past summer
3. The children go to the <u>neighborhood</u> schools. They go to _____ schools.
4. She is in a habit of reading <u>rapidly</u>. She is a _____ reader.
5. Dorothy was <u>ill</u> during last week. Her _____ lasted one week.
6. She is <u>doing</u> some chores around the house. She _____ around the house.
7. Her father <u>bought</u> Dorothy a new dress. He went to town to _____ a dress for Dorothy.
8. Mr. Axby waits until his children <u>come</u> <u>out</u> of school. He waits for his children _____ _____ school.
9. This happens on <u>days</u> <u>when</u> <u>it</u> <u>rains</u>. It happens during _____ _____.
10. Mr. Axby cannot find a <u>place</u> <u>to</u> <u>park</u> He cannot find _____ _____.

PROGRESS EVALUATION

Let's Continue
(Chapters 1-5)

1. Write another word for the two-word verb. Select the <u>right</u> word from the words given below:

create   pay a visit   happen   test   mention
quit   depend   discuss   deliver   fetch

a. pick up _____.
b. go on_____.
c. turn over_____.
d. come over_____.
e. work up_____.

f. give up _____.
g. count on _____.
h. talk over _____.
i. try on _____.
j. bring up _____.

2. Fill in the missing word in the dialogue. Use the words given below.

     known   sorry   honor   obey   interrupt   have

J: All motorists must _____ the speed limits.
S: But, your _____.
J. You should not _____ while I speak.
S: I am _____, your honor.
J. You should _____ been more careful while driving.
S: I should've _____ better!

3. Identify the <u>function</u> of the <u>modal perfect.</u>
    Example: He <u>should have paid attention.</u>   <u>   advisability   </u>

a. You <u>should have been</u> more careful.   _____
b. They <u>could have seen </u>another car.   _____
c. You <u>must have been </u>speeding.   _____

d. You <u>can't have done</u> this already. _____
e. My friend <u>may have told</u> a lie. _____

4. Choose a two-word verb from the verbs listed and write it on the blank line.

going on   pick up   give up   bring back   work up
count on   try on   talk over keep on   turn off

a. You forgot to <u>return</u> _____ my football.
b. O.K., I <u>surrender</u> _____.
c. Let's <u>create</u> _____ an appetite!
d. I'll <u>fetch</u> _____ the ball tomorrow.
e. Hey, what's <u>happening</u> _____?
f. You can always <u>depend</u> _____ a good friend.
g. Tomorrow, I'll <u>test</u> _____a new warm-up suit.
h. And don't forget to <u>make a turn</u> _____at San Pedro Ave.
i. We'll <u>discuss</u> _____ it later.
j. We must <u>continue</u> _____ to exercise.

5. Select the right word to complete the sentence.

human   body   incurable   vigor   person
art   nourishment exercise   popular   balance

a. Everybody admires the _____ of youth.
b. We like to maintain a healthy _____.
c. The _____ body requires good care.
d. Aging is an _____ disease.
e. People must _____ regularly.
f. A _____ must keep up the daily conditioning.
g. A _____ form of exercise is jogging.
h. The body must receive sufficient _____.
i. We look for a _____ between the body and the mind.
j. It is important for a person to appreciate _____.

6. Select the correct two-word verb and substitute it in the line next to the underlined word in the sentence.

beware of   account for   wait for   asked for   wish for
be aware of   refer to   look at   looks like   argue with

a. I <u>inquired about</u> _____ a good dentist.
b. Can I <u>delay</u> _____ the treatment?
c. How do you <u>explain</u> _____ the cavities?
d. We must <u>be watchful</u> of _____ misusing the car.
e. Let me <u>inspect</u> _____ your tooth.
f. This <u>seems</u> _____ like we're having trouble.
g. We <u>call</u> _____ this environmental pollution.
h. I don't <u>disagree</u> _____ with you, doctor.
i. We must <u>recognize</u> _____ our environment.
j. Let's not <u>want</u> _____ a dirty environment.

7. Lexical Units

Select the word(s) or phrase(s) from the words listed below that best complete(s) each of the sentences. One selection may be used more than once. Read the sentences aloud.

Example: Air is an important element.
              Everybody needs to <u>breathe.</u>

allow   pure   unhealthy   guard
automobile   plant   keep   especially
depends   pollution   need

1. People cannot survive without air. We _____ clean air.
2. Our environment is the place in which all of us live. We must _____ our environment clean.
3. In a mechanized world, it is difficult to keep the air clean. It is _____ difficult in large cities.
4. When we make air dirty, it is unsafe for breathing. We must _____against making our environment _____ to live in.

5. People need a car to move from place to place. The automobile is a major cause of air _____.

6. We need this means of transportation. But we need our air more than we need the _____.

7. We have ourselves to blame for it, if we _____ our environment to become unsafe.

8. People argue on many issues. They must agree on one: all life _____ on clean air.

9. People need to become nature lovers. This means that we have to _____ trees and plants.

10. Trees and plants are necessary. They keep the air _____.

PROGRESS EVALUATION

Let's Continue
(Chapters 6-10)

1. Dictation

a. _____.
b. _____.
c. _____.
d. _____.
e. _____.

2. Guess what would happen if things had occurred differently in the following circumstances,

Example: <u>We're invited to a boat party. But we arrive late and the boat has sailed without us.</u>
<u>If we arrived in time for the party, we would sail on the boat.</u>

a. We were careless, and we received a traffic ticket. _____
   _____

b. We were late, and the party began without us. _____
   _____

c. We didn't study, and we failed the exam. _____
   _____

d. We hurried to school, and we forgot our books. _____
   _____

e. We didn't save money, and now we can't buy the car we need. _____

3. Lexical Units

Select the word from the words listed below that best completes each of the sentences. One selection may be used more than once. Read the sentences aloud.

Example: If we get home early, we watch the news.
Everybody needs to be informed.

more	expensive	understood
gratitude	had	knew
didn't	peaceful	unhappy
satisfied	people	would
ask		

a. Someone tells you that you may make a wish. You will probably _____ for something that you like.
b. If your parents are wealthy, you'll probably ask for an_____car.
c. Being wealthy does not guarantee happiness. Many wealthy persons are _____.
d. You will have no trouble if you lead an unpretentious life. An unpretentious life is _____.
e. Oftentimes, we wish we had many things we don't need. That's how _____ are.
f. When we understand life only a little, we wish we _____more.
g. We know things pretty well, now. We wish we _____everything better.
h. When we have something, we always wish we _____more of it.
i. It is safe to assume that persons who always want more that they possess will remain _____.
j. If they lived in a small house, they _____ want it to be bigger.
k. If they had a big home, they would be _____.
l. Happiness depends on the way we see the world. If we _____ look at _____ our world with _____ for all things we have, we would remain _____ forever.
m. Supposing you had all you wished for, would you wish for _____.

4. TRANSFORM THE FOLLOWING SENTENCES INTO THE *passive voice*:

a. Martha bought a dress.

_____.

b. Carl drives the car.

_____.

c. The thief stole my wallet.

_____.

d. The police caught the thief.

_____.

e. Akira examined the suits.

_____.

5. Underline the PASSIVE VOICE and tell the TENSE.

tense

a. The house was finally completed.   _____
b. Work is being done.   _____
c. A strike was organized.   _____
d. They'll be taken to school.   _____
e. Milk has been donated by the county. _____

ACHIEVEMENT EVALUATION

Let's Begin

1. Listen and write (page 259 of Text).

   a. _____
   b. _____
   c. _____
   d. _____

2. Use of <u>a</u> or <u>some</u>.

   Example: Please give me <u>some</u> milk.

   a. Hiromi has _____ book.
   b. Ann buys _____ pen.
   c. There's _____ soap in the bathroom.
   d. Let's go and buy _____ milk.
   e. The child plays on _____ carpet.
   f. He's standing under _____ tree.
   g. Don't you have _____ dish for the food?
   h. Ann puts _____ cream into the coffee.
   i. Louis asks for _____ toothpaste.
   j. They're buying _____ carpets.

3. Completion
   Complete the <u>TALK</u> using the words below.

   in front of * next * wonderful * above * extra * bathroom

   Louis: What's _____ the garage?
   Angel: Oh, that's an _____ room.

Manuel: An _____ room? That's _____!
Bertha: What's _____ to the room?
Angel: It's my _____.
Louis: You're _____? How about a car?
Angel: My car's _____ _____ _____ the garage.

4. Complete the reading using the words below.

downstaris   *   on top of   *   bedroom(s)   *   upstairs
             in front of   *   next to

There are three _____ in our house. One _____
_____ is _____ the first floor. One bathroom is _____
_____. Another bathroom is _____. The garage is
the house. There is an extra room _____ the garage. There
are some trees _____ the house.

Suggested Method Of
Achievement Evaluation Of Oral Competence

(Level *Zero-Plus* to *One*)

1. Common courtesies:

How are you?
What's your name?
What do you do?
Do you have a car?
Who's your friend?
What do you like to eat?
What do you like to drink?
Do you study a lot?
Do you like picnics?
When do you go on picnics?
Etc., etc.

ACHIEVEMENT EVALUATION

Let's Converse

Aural comprehension examination (chapters 6-10). The teacher reads aloud, and the students circle the correct answers.

1. Circle (a., b., or c.) the correct sentence.

   a. I been waiting for you.
   b. I have been waiting for you.
   c. I has been waiting for you.

   a. He has been thinking of it.
   b. He thinking of it.
   c. He been thinking of it.

   a. She had been eaten.
   b. She had eaten.
   c. She been eaten.

   a. They have driving home.
   b. They have drove home.
   c. They have driven home.

   a. You had invite him.
   b. You had invited him.
   c. You had inviting him.

   a. Arturo hasn't been here.
   b. Arturo haven't been here.
   c. Arturo have been here.

a. Minoo had been jumping.
b. Minoo been jumping.
c. Minoo have been jumping.

a. He had flying all day.
b. He had been flying all day.
c. He have flying all day.

2. Circle (a., b., or c.) the correct response to the question.

Can't you come tonight?

a. No, I can't.
b. No, we can't.
c. Yes, I can't.

Should she go to school?

a. Yes, she should.
b. Yes, she could.
c. Yes, she shouldn't.

Won't you stay?

a. No, I won't stay.
b. No, I won't say.
c. No, I'll stay.

Would he like to order?

a. No, he would.
b. Yes, he would.
c. Yes, he wouldn't.

Must I eat this?

a. Yes, she must.
b. Yes, you musn't.
c. Yes, you must.

Couldn't they leave?

a. No, they could.
b. No, they couldn't.
c. No, we couldn't.

Shall we go?

a. Yes, you shall.
b. Yes, they shall.
c. Yes, we shall.

Will you remember?

a. Yes, I'll will.
b. Yes, I will.
c. Yes, will 1.

3. Circle (a., b., or c.) the correct sentence.

a. She made a good grade except that she studied.
b. She made a good grade because she studied.
c. She made a good grade although she studied.

a. We'll meet as soon as they close.
b. We'll meet as soon as they closed.
c. We'll meet as soon as they closes.

a. They are yet shopping.
b. They are until shopping.
c. They are still shopping.

a. He has already gone.
b. He has lately gone.
c. He hasn't finally gone.

4. The students will give the correct spelling for each word they hear.

    a.   f.

    b.   g.

    c.   h.

    d.   i.

    e.   j.

5. Fill in the missing preposition for each blank.

    a. She waited _____ me _____ the store.

    b. I will wait _____ noon.

    c. He will think _____ it.

    d. They came back _____ their vacation yesterday.

    e. Ali listened _____ his teacher.

    f. I'll finish the homework _____ the morning.

    g. She tried _____ the coat.

    h. Amelia went _____ bus.

    i. He slept _____ the movie.

Suggested Method Of
Achievement Evaluation Of Oral Competence

(Level One Plus to Two)

1. General courtesies:

    "How are you?"
    "How's your family?"
    "Are you having fun?"
    "What do you do on weekends?" Etc., etc.

2. Questions of biographical nature:

    "What's your name?"
    "Do you have a large family?"
    "How many sisters?"
    "Brothers?" Etc., etc.

3. Subject of study:

   "What are you studying?"
   "What do you wish to become ?"
   "Is anyone in your family a _____?" Etc., etc.

4. Develop further, if necessary, with reference to grammar sophistication and vocabulary discrimination.

ACHIEVEMENT EVALUATION

Let's Read
(Chapter 8)

A. Substitute, where possible, the synonym of the word underlined.
   Example: His family likes the new <u>position</u>.
              His family was happy when he had gotten the new
              ___job___ .

1. The professor had been <u>shopping</u> for a job._____
2. The Stuarts went to <u>select</u> a house._____
3. John was <u>trying</u> to improve his knowledge._____
4. It was larger than the one they <u>required</u>._____
5. They <u>established</u> a friendship._____
6. Moving is always a great <u>chore</u>._____
7. They <u>planned</u> a neighborhood party._____
8. The only <u>problem</u> was Mrs. Fox._____
9. Everyone <u>dropped</u> in to celebrate._____
10. Mrs. Fox suddenly <u>understood</u>._____

B. Select the word (a., b., or c.) that best fits the meaning of the first
   word given.

1. appropriate	a. grumpy	b. proper	c. improper
2. better	a. improve	b. worsen	c. learn
3. difficulty	a. problem	b. task	c. solution
4. embrace	a. recoil	b. hug	c. possess
5. express regret	a. blame	b. apologize	c. resolve
6. have faith	a. hold on	b. trust	c. mistrust
7. imposing	a. unimpressive	b. impressive	c. unafraid
8. next	a. previous	b. following	c. modest
9. offer	a. present	b. say	c. withhold
10. perplex	a. relieve	b. relax	c. confuse
11. redeem	a. save	b. lose	c. own

12. secure   a. break up   b. establish   c. move
13. select   a. sell   b. shop   c. bring
14. sincerely   a. heartily   b. distant   c. insincerely
15. trade for   a. take   b. sell   c. buy
    money

C. Circle the word in Column II most <u>LIKE</u> the word in Column I, and circle the word in Column III most <u>UNLIKE</u> the word in Column I.

<u>I</u>

1. afford:	II	a. have the money for	b. practice	c. list
	III	a. need	b. misbehave	c. retain
2. apologize:	II	a. declare	b. express regret	c. testify
	III	a. repress	b. be wrong	c. blame
3. decide:	II	a. resolve	b. testify	c. affirm
	III	a. precede	b. hesitate	c. avoid
4. embarrass:	II	a. dominate	b. perplex	c. separate
	III	a. relieve	b. advise	c. counsel
5. establish:	II	a. control	b. secure	c. detain
	III	a. let go	b. tip over	c. break up
6. following:	II	a. beyond	b. next	c. farther
	III	a. previous	b. next	c. orderly
7. heartily:	II	a. sincerely	b. sympathetic	c. kind
	III	a. court	b. unkind	c. insincere
8. impressive:	II	a. wealthy	b. imposing	c. protected
	III	a. unimpressive	b. unsafe	c. usual
9. improve:	II	a. rest	b. better	c. listen
	III	a. hinder	b. worsen	c. lick
10. minor:	II	a. secondary	b. happy	c. grumpy
	III	a. at rest	b. major	c. active
11. problem:	II	a. opportunity	b. chore	c. different
	III	a. solution	b. task	c. trust
12. proper:	II	a. modest	b. appropriate	c. simple
	III	a. improper	b. protected	c. distant
13. save:	II	a. assure	b. succeed	c. redeem
	III	a. lose	b. ignore	c. dominate

14. sell:	II	a. sink	b. work	c. trade for money
	III	a. buy	b. stop	c. rest
15. shop:	II	a. cross	b. behave	c. select
	III	a. work	b. take	c. sell

D. Fill in the word (phrase) most fitting to express the concept of the sentence according to the narrative.

1. The Stuart family was happy when the professor _____.
   a. got a position   b. met the Campbells
   c. learned Chinese   d. looked for a job

2. John Stuart knew his knowledge of Chinese was _____.
   a. as good as Lilian's   b. not as good as Lilian's
   c. better than Lilian's   d. as good as it could be

3. He worked hard to _____.
   a. improve his friendship   b. be a good chairman
   c. improve his knowledge   d. learn more about Lilian
   of the language

4. They bought a bigger house than they needed because _____.
   a. the Foxes lived there.   b. they liked the neighborhood
   c. they met at social   d. Lilian liked to give parties
   gatherings

5. Some neighbors helped the Stuarts with their moving because _____.
   a. they liked the Campbells   b. they were next door neighbors.
   c. moving is a great chore   d. they studied at M.Y.U.

6. With her remark, Mrs. Fox showed _____.
   a. her prejudice   b. her friendship
   c. her worry   d. her happiness

7. The Campbells were worried because the Stuarts might be
_____.

   a. hurt by the prejudice   b. afraid

   b. accustomed to prejudice   d. prejudiced Like Mrs. Fox

8. Lilian waited five years in residence to recive her citizenship
because _____.

   a. she was in Taiwan   b. she studied at M.Y.U.

   c. she liked the   d. it is the required time
      United States

9. Mrs. Campbell cried at the ceremony because it _____.

   a. took a long time   b. was required

   c. was impressive   d. was the twentieth of May

10. The Stuarts planned a big party to _____.

   a. celebrate Lilian's   b. invite Mrs. Fox
      citizenship

   c. invite unfriendly   d. have fun
      neighbors

11. Lilian planned the party when _____.

   a. it was her birthday   b. the Foxes were away

   c. John was at the College   d. and Shawn were at school

12. Mrs. Fox appeared at the Stuart's home to _____.

   a. come to the party   b. apologize for missing the
      party

   c. be prejudiced   d. speak to John

13. Lilian was happy because she knew that _____.

   a. her party was not in vain   b. Mrs. Fox was prejudiced

   c. she gave a good party   d. John was happy

14. Lilian gave Mrs. Fox a chance to _____.

   a. worry   b. be happy

   c. be away   d. save face

15. Mrs. Fox realized that Lilian _____.
    a. really cared for people   b. was from Taiwan
    c. loved John   d. gave good parties

E. Place a check mark in front of the correct response to each of the statements according to the narrative:

1. The Stuarts were
   happy because
       ___a. the professor signed with the college.
       ___b. they were moving.
       ___c. they bought a house.

2. After John signed
   with the college
       ___a. they gave a party.
       ___b. they went to shop for a house.
       ___c. they took a trip.

3. John met Lilian
       ___a. when they were students at M.Y.U.
       ___b. when he was in Taiwan.
       ___c. when she visited in the United States.

4. The Stuarts went
   out to
       ___a. move.
       ___b. shop for a house.
       ___c. plan a party.

5. They moved not
   far from
       ___a. the Campbells.
       ___b. the college.
       ___c. the neighborhood.

6. The professor and
   Mrs. Campbell
   studied
       ___a. in Taiwan.
       ___b. at M.Y.U.
       ___c. law.

7. The neighbors
   helped the Stuarts
       ___a. at the college.
       ___b. with the party.
       ___c. with the moving.

8. Lilian planned the
   party when

   ___a. the Foxes were away.
   ___b. the neighbors would come.
   ___c. the Campbells would come.

9. When the Foxes
   returned, Mrs. Fox

   ___a. cane to talk with John.
   ___b. came to the party.
   ___c. came to apologize to Lilian.

10. Lilian wanted to
    give Mrs. Fox a
    chance to

   ___a. come to the party.
   ___b. save face.
   ___c. be present.

F. Write T for True in front of each statement that you think is true. Write F for False if the statement is not true.

___1. Professor Stuart got a job, and his family was happy.
___2. The professor had been looking for a job since February.
___3. He was offered the position of chairman.
___4. The Stuarts had two sons.
___5. Lilian was of Chinese descent.
___6. The house was not very expensive.
___7. Moving is easy.
___8. The Stuarts had been accustomed to prejudice.
___9. Lilian received her citizenship in March.
___10. Mr. Campbell sponsored Lilian.
___11. The Stuarts planned a big party.
___12. Mrs. Fox was no problem.
___13. Lilian gave the party when the Foxes were home.
___14. The party was a great success.
___15. Everyone missed the Foxes.
___16. Mrs. Fox came to apologize for missing the party.
___17. Lilian was glad about Mrs. Fox's visit.
___18. Mrs. Fox and Lilian were going to be friends.
___19. Mrs. Fox embraced Lilian.
___20. The Stuarts moved on Monday.

G. In Column I are the beginnings of sentences. In Column II are the completions to sentences of Column I. Select the completion best fitting each sentence in Column I according to the narrative.

Column I	Column II
____1. The professor had been looking	a. for a proper occasion
____2. He was glad	b. about the Stuarts.
____3. The Stuarts went out	c. while they were students.
____4. John Married Lilian	d. when he was offered a position.
____5. Lilian was a student	e. for a job since January.
____6. It was larger than	f. a great chore.
____7. John and Lilian	g. you must really care for people.
____8. Moving is always	h. what the Stuarts needed.
____9. Why don't these foreigners	i. from Taiwan.
____10. The Campbells were worried	j. to welcome the new American.
____11. Lilian received her citizenship	k. a great success.
____12. The Stuarts planned	1. Mrs. Fox appeared at the Stuarts.
____13. They had been waiting	m. to be friends now.
____14. The party was	n. to shop for a house.
____15. Everyone was happy	o. liked the neighborhood.
____16. On the following day	p. stay out of our neighborhood?
____17. To do a thing like this	q. on the twentieth of May.
____18. They were going	r. a big party to celebrate.

ACHIEVEMENT EVALUATION
Let's Write
(Chapter 2)
Part One: Mechanics

1. Fill in the blank spaces to complete the following sentences:

    a. The three types of paragraphs in a composition are the
   _____, _____ and the _____.

    b. A complex sentence has one _____ clause and one or
   more _____ _____.

    c. In a complex sentence the dependent clause is introduced by
   means of _____.

    d. The four forms of writing are _____, _____,
   _____, and _____.

    e. The main idea in a paragraph is expressed in the _____
   _____.

2. Write a complete sentence for each word(s):

    a. however   _____

    b. besides   _____

    c. although   _____

    d. as soon as   _____

    e. unless   _____

3. Write a sentence using the following verbs in the tense next
to the verb:

    a. study   (present perfect) _____

    b. eat   (past perfect) _____

    c. drive (present perfect) _____

    d. walk (past perfect) _____

    e. fly   (past perfect progressive) _____

Part Two: Structure

Summary Of Parts Of Speech. Fill in the missing form of the word:

Example:

Noun	Verb	Adjective	Adverb
economy	economize	economical	economically
	dramatize		
		hopeful	
			memorably
reversal			
	evade		
	success		
			satisfactorily
consideration			
	separate		

Supply The Missing <u>Preposition</u> For Each Blank Space:

1. Ads come _____ different forms.
2. Products are announced _____ TV and radio.
3. Many agencies furnish a variety _____ services.
4. Short films are produced _____ advertising.
5. Haven't you heard _____ MATADOR cereal?
6. I've heard _____ it now and then.
7. The advertiser exaggerates _____ the merchandise.
8. The consumer falls victim _____ advertising.
9. Millions _____ people buy advertised products.
10. Most manufacturers stand _____ their products.
11. This is the way _____ free enterprise.
12. He worked _____ midnight.
13. She listened _____him.
14. I haven't seen him _____ yesterday.
15. Mary waited _____ John.

Subject-Verb Agreement -- Underline The Correct Verb Form.

1. Advertising (is/are) an American way of life.
2. People (is/are) consumers.
3. Merchants (buy/buys) ads for their products.
4. Ads (come/comes) in different ways.

Transformations -- Transform The Following Sentences:

1. Advertising is a way of life.
2. America likes advertising.
3. The advertisers are manufacturers.
4. Merchants buy ads for their products.

Completeness/Write A Complete Sentence For Each Of The Following Fragments:

1. are manufacturers

2. buy ads for their products

3. are many ways to advertise

4. carry advertisements

Write One Paragraph Consisting Of At Least Eight (8) to Ten (10) Sentences. Choose One Title:

A Day In The Zoo
How I Change A Flat Tire
The Person I Love
How I Say Goodbye To My Date

ACHIEVEMENT EVALUATION

Let's Continue
(Chapter 1)

1. Write another word for the two word verb. Select the right word from the words given below.

create	pay a visit	happen	test	mention
quit	depend	discuss	deliver	fetch

a. pick up   _____   f. give up   _____
b. go on   _____   g. count on   _____
c. turn over   _____   h. talk over   _____
d. come over   _____   i. try on   _____
e. work up   _____   j. bring up   _____

2. Choose a two-word verb from the verbs listed and write it on the blank line.

going	* pick up *	give up	* bring back *	work up
count on	* try on *	talk over	* keep on *	turn off

a. You forgot to <u>return</u> _____ my football.
b. O.K., I <u>surrender</u> _____.
c. Let's <u>create</u> _____ an appetite!
d. I'll <u>fetch</u> _____ the ball tomorrow.
e. Hey, what's <u>happening</u> _____?
f. You can always <u>depend</u> _____ on a good friend.
g. Tomorrow, I'll <u>test</u> _____ a new warm-up suit.
h. And don't forget to <u>make a turn</u> _____ at San Pedro Ave.
i. We'll <u>discuss</u> _____ it later.
j. We must <u>continue</u> _____ to exercise.

3. Select the right word to complete the sentence.

>   human   *   body   *   incurable * vigor * person
>   art   *   exercise *   popular   * nourishment * balance

>   a. Everybody admires the _____ of youth.
>   b. We like to maintain a healthy _____.
>   c. The _____ body requires good care.
>   d. Aging is an _____ disease.
>   e. People must _____ regularly.
>   f. A _____ must keep up the daily conditioning.
>   g. A _____ form of exercise is jogging.
>   h. The body must receive sufficient _____.
>   i. We look for a _____ between the body and the mind.
>   j. It is important for a person to appreciate _____.

4. Fill in the proper word.

>   a. Only a short time ago, people tr_____ on horseback.
>   b. People always dr_____ of flying.
>   c. Failure did not dis_____ the inventors.
>   d. The biggest obstacle was gr_____.
>   e. The invention of the steam engine changed so_____.

5. Change the present tense to simple past tense.

>   a. We study every day.

>   _____

>   b. Evelyn is a very good astronaut.

>   _____

>   c. Life gets more difficult each day.

>   _____

>   d. The little girl falls on her face.

>   _____

>   e. I fly to Dallas every month.

>   _____

6. Fill in the missing word in the dialogue. Use the words given below.

   known * sorry * honor * obey * interrupt * have

   J. All motorists must _____ the speed limit.
   S: But, your _____.
   J. You should not _____ while I speak.
   S: I am _____, your honor.
   J. You should _____ been more careful while driving.
   S: I should've _____ better.

7. Select the right <u>model</u> to complete the sentence. You can use the same word more than once.

   may * must * would * night * will * should
   could * can

   a. You _____ have been more careful. (advisability)
   b. He _____ have paid attention. (advisability)
   c. She _____n't have driven so fast. (advisability)
   d. At least they _____ have warned me. (advisability)
   e. Max _____ have told me about the speed trap.
                                                (conditioned result)
   f. I _____ have avoided the ticket.
                                                (conditioned result)

8. The following sentences are all in the **Conditional**. Select the right word and write it in the sentence which you think needs this word.

   have * will * I'll * can * knew * lived * read
   would * learned * are

   a If we reach the planets, there _____ many surprises.
   b. If I'm selected, _____ go.
   c. If we _____ be happy, provided I _____ return.
   d. If you_____ the money, you _____ be happy.
   e. If we _____ about it, we _____ be better prepared.
   f. We wish we _____ it better.
   g. If we _____ in Africa, we _____ know alot about
      its people.

h. If they _____ in a small house, they _____ want a bigger one.

i. If we _____ more, we _____ be happier.

j. We wish we _____ English.

9. Lexical Units Select one word for each sentence that best completes each sentence. Choose from the words listed below. One selection may be used more than once.

   Example: If we get home early, we watch the news.
            Everybody needs to be informed.

more	expensive	understood
gratitude	had	knew
satisfied	peaceful	unhappy
didn't	people	would
ask		

   a. Someone tells you that you may make a wish. You will probably _____ for something that you like.

   b. If your parents are wealthy, you'll probably ask for an _____ car.

   c. Being wealthy does not guarantee happiness. Many wealthy persons are _____ .

   d. You will have no trouble if you lead an unpretentious life. An unpretentious life is _____.

   e. Oftentimes, we wish we had many things we don't need. That's now _____ are.

   f. When we understand life only a little, we wish we _____ more.

   g. We know things pretty well, now. We wish we _____ even better.

   h. When we have something, we always wish we _____ more of it.

   i. It is safe to assume that persons who always want more than they possess will remain _____.

   j. If they lived in a small house, they _____ want it to be bigger.

   k. If they had a big home, they would be _____.

   l. Happiness depends in the way we see the world. If we

_____ look at our world with _____ for all things we have, we would remain _____ forever.

m. Supposing you had all you wished for, would you wish for

_____.

10. Finish the sentence by selecting the <u>if</u>-clause that describes a <u>past condition</u>. (countrary to fact). Read the sentences aloud.

Example: Even if Gloria had eaten well,
           a. she wouldn't be pretty.
           b. she wouldn't have been pretty.

<u>Even if Gloria had eaten well, she wouldn't have been pretty</u>.

a. Even if we had told a lie,

    1) we wouldn't be sorry.
    2) we wouldn't have been sorry.

b. If Ytaka had studied harder,

    1) he wouldn't fail the test.
    2) he wouldn't have failed the test.

c. If we had lived many thousands of years ago,

    1) we would have acted the same way as our ancestors did.
    2) we would act the same way as our ancestors did.

d. If we had inhabited arid land,

    1) we would have fought wars to gain fertile land.
    2) we would fight wars to gain fertile land.

e. They could have grown much food

    1) if they had gained fertile.
    2) if they gained fertile land.

f. We would not have killed them

　　1) if we had wished for people to accept our faith.
　　2) if we wished for people to accept our faith.

_____

g. If we had wanted to impress others,

　　1) we would impress them with our kindness.
　　2) we would have impressed them with our kindness.

_____

h. If I were a leader,

　　1) I would love all of my people.
　　2) I would have loved all of my people.

_____

i. If we had educated the people,

　　1) knowledge would have liberated them from fear.
　　2) knowledge would li berate them from fear.

_____

j. If we had borrowed money from the bank,

　　1) we would have returned it by now.
　　2) we would return it by now.

_____

11. Transform the following sentences into the <u>passive</u> voice:

a. Martha bought a dress.

_____

b. Carl drives the car.

_____

c. The thief stole my wallet.

_____

d. The police caught the thief.

_____

e. Akira examined the suits.

_____

12. Underline the <u>passive</u> voice and tell the <u>tense</u>.

tense

   a. The house was finally completed.   _____

   b. Work is being done.   _____

   c. A strike was organized.   _____

   d. They'll be taken to school.   _____

   e. Milk has been donated by the country.   _____

13. Write a composition (three paragraphs) about one topic.

   a. One day in my life.

   b. What I like in the United States.

   c. My family.

   d. The person I admire most.

SUGGESTED METHOD OF
ACHIEVEMENT/EVALUATION FOR ORAL COMPETENCE

(*Level Two-Plus to Three*)

1. Adopt the context of the interview to the individual's purpose.

2. Conduct the interview at first on a <u>basic</u> survival level; escalate to <u>social</u> questions of general context, such as questions of biographical nature, general information concerning the examinee and those he wishes to discuss.

3. Continue interview with reference to current news, allowing examinee to express personal views.

4. Enter questions concerning examinee's plans and activities, be they professional or pre-professional.

5. Consult with examinee on certain simple problems, such as:

> "I have a problem --- I work too hard."
> I don't see my family often enough."
> My car didn't start this morning."
> My oldest child is ill."
> I wake up at night with this nagging headache."

Sustain the dialogue and disagree on different issues with the examinee.

6. Finally, to evaluate maximum competence, confront the examinee with some "repair" problems:

   a. "How would you go about having your wristwatch repaired? Appraise and report?"

   b. "You want to travel around the world. Call a travel agency and get all the details."

   c. "The bathtub drainage doesn't work. Call the plumbers and have it repaired."

   d. Think of other unusual situations you could exploit.

   Any evaluation properly conducted ought to demonstrate the breath and limitations of the examinee's competence in a given area of the language. It should serve as an indicator of the teacher's past achievements and future course outline.

ADDITIONAL SAMPLE EVALUATIONS

Let's Begin
Chapter Seven—Sample test

Listen and **Write**

coffee _____ good _____ fresh _____.
This coffee is good. _____
It is fresh. _____
Where _____ are _____ eggs _____
Where are the eggs? _____
loaf _____ sliced _____ bread _____
A loaf of sliced bread. _____

Write a **Dialogue** about the following situation.
You are in a supermarket.
You ask the baker for a loaf of bread.
He asks you how you like it.
You tell him you like it sliced.
He gives you the bread.
You thank him.
He says good-bye.
You say good-bye.

Change sentences as in the example.
   Example: This is a banana. (yellow)
               The banana is yellow.
               It is yellow.

This is an apple. (red)

_____

This is a loaf of bread. (brown)

_____

That's a coat. (black)

_____

This is my shirt. (green)

_____

That's her jacket. (blue)

_____

Example: These are Louis' jackets. (brown)
         These are Louis' brown jackets.
         They're brown.

These are bananas. (yellow)

_____

There are apples on the shelf. (red)

_____

Ann has two eyes. (blue)

_____

These are my shoes. (black)

_____

Those are Louis' pants. (green)

_____

Let's Converse
Chapter Six—Sample test

Perfect Tense & Past Participles

Part I, Multiple-Choice: Circle the correct answer.

1. Did you write a love letter? Yes, I _____ a love letter.
   a. writed   b. wrote   c. written   d. writ

2. They have _____ (make) good cars this year.
   a. make   b. maked   c. made   d. mad

3. Oh! Mr. Banford has _____ (see) a snake!
   a. seed   b. seen   c. saw   d. said

4. Yes, Mary, they have _____ (take) a vacation.
   a. took   b. taken   c.taked   d. talked

5. No, they _____ (go) to Chinatown yet.
   a. have gone   b. haven't   c. are going   d. gone
                     gone

Part II, Slashed Sentences: Combine the following words to form a <u>correct</u> sentence.

6. I/already/eat (past participle) /have/breakfast

7. usually/go/John/at 8o'clock/to school

8. Mr. Banford/never/tennis/play

Part III, Fill-Ins: Fill in the blanks with the correct form of "get"

9. Yes, the cirminal _____ _____ (escaped).

10. Mary always _____ excited when she has a test.

Part IV, Complete Answers: Answer the following questions with complete answers.

11. How often does Mr. Banford brush his teeth? (sometimes)
12. When did you arrive here? (Use "get")

Part V, Sentence Correction: This is a bad sentence. Change it to a good sentence.

13. I am living in San Antonio for six months.

Let's Read
Chapter Two—Sample test

Part I. If the following words have the same meaning, put an "S" between them. If they are different in meaning, put an "0" between them.

a. typical _____ unusual
b. lose _____ gain
c. yell _____ shout
d. own _____ possess
e. discomfort _____ annoyance
f. near _____ distant
g. area _____ spot
h. camping _____ outing

Part II. Fill in the blanks below with an appropriate word to complete the sentence.

The Campbells are a _____ American _____. Mr. Campbell is a _____. He _____ as a lawyer. Mrs. Campbell is a housewife. She _____ what she does.

The Campbells _____ an _____ cabin. The countryside in La Grange is. _____. The Colorado River _____ through _____ _____. This makes up for the _____ of the _____ quarters.

Part III. Make A Sentence Using The Following Words.

a. wet _____

b. fetch _____

c. respond _____

d. toast _____

Let's Write
Chapter Two—Sample test

Place the correct end punctuation at the close of each sentence below. On the line tell what kind of thought the sentence expresses (Declarative, Imperative Interrogative, Exclamatory).

Example: Show me the picture.   *Imperative*

1. The National Air and Space Museum
   is in our nation's capital

2. The Smithsonian Institution is in
   Washington, D.C. isn't it   _____

3. The Smithsonian is an amazing place.   _____

4. Stop that immediately   _____

5. Please close the door   _____

6. Does San Antonio have a mild climate   _____

7. The price of the car seemed fair   _____

8. Did you have to walk a long distance to
   get here   _____

9. Mr. Campbell is an attorney-at-law   _____

10. Is Mrs. Campbell going on vacation
    with the family   _____

Subject Verb Agreement

Underline the correct form of the verb below.

1. Advertising (is/are) an American way of life.
2. America (need/needs) advertising.
3. People (is/are) consumers.
4. The advertisers (is/are) manufacturers.

5. Merchants (buy/buys) ads for their products.
6. Advertising (mean/means) success.
7. Ads (come/comes) in different ways.
8. Newspapers (carries/carry) advertisements.
9. Many agencies (furnish/furnishes) a variety of services.

Define the following terms:

1. Paragraph =
2. Sentence =
3. Subject =
4. Verb =
5. Topic Sentence =

Underline the sentence in the paragraph below that does not belong because it breaks the paragraph unity.

A simple electromagnet can be made by wrapping insulated wire around a spool, then sticking a long spike or bolt up through the hole. When the ends of the wire are attached to the poles of a battery and a current is sent through the coils around the spool, the spike inside the spool is made magnetic. It loses its magnetism, however, as soon as the current is stopped. Benjamin Franklin flew a kite in a thunderstorm and drew electricity down the string.

Write ten simple sentences below.

1. _____
2. _____
3. _____
4. _____
5. _____
6. _____
7. _____
8. _____
9. _____
10. _____

Let's Continue
Chapter One—Sample test

1. Write another word for the two word verb. Select the <u>right</u> word from the words given below:

create	pay a visit	happen	test	mention
quit	depend	discuss	deliver	fetch

a. pick up _____ f. give up _____

b. go on _____ g. count on _____

c. turn over _____ h. talk over _____

d. come over _____ i. try on _____

e. work up _____ j. bring up _____

2. Rewrite the sentences and use two word verbs in place of the <u>underlined</u> words.

1. Please, <u>return</u> my football.

2. <u>Be glad</u>, Jason, it isn't as bad as all that!
   _____

3. You can <u>depend</u> on it, my friend.
   _____

4. The thief <u>surrenders to</u> the police.
   _____

5. Hi, Robert, what's <u>happening</u>?
   _____

6. With proper exercise, we <u>anticipate</u> a long and healthy life.
   _____

7. I'm going to <u>examine</u> some of the suits.
   _____

8. His friend will <u>repay</u> him tomorrow.
   _____

9. The longer you <u>postpone</u> exercising, the more difficult it will be to start with the program.
   _____

10. A person exercises to <u>remove</u> some weight.
    _____

Let's Converse
Chapter Two— Sample Test for *Oral Comprehension*
(*To Be Read By Teacher*)

Circle The Correct **Plural**:

A. This is an assignment.
 1. These are assignments.
 2. They is assignments.
 3. These is assignment.

B. This is a dog.
 1. They is dogs.
 2. These are dogs
 3. These is dogs.

C. This is a test.
 1. This are tests.
 2. They is tests.
 3. These are tests.

D. This is a boy.
 1. They are a boy.
 2. These are boys.
 3. They is boys.

E. This is city.
 1. These are cities.
 2. They is cities.
 3. These is cities.

Circle The Correct Frequency **Word** Reply:

A. How often does it rain?
 1. It rains on Sunday.
 2. It usually rains on Sunday.
 3. It rains tomorrow.

B. Do you ever play?
 1. I sometimes play.
 2. I play on Monday.
 3. I play on Weekends.

C. Does she always study?
 1. She studies on weekends.
 2. She studies on Friday
 3. No, not always,

 .

D. Is he ever on time?
 1. Yes, he's usually on time.
 2. No, he's there on Mon day.
 3. Yes, he's here on weekends.

E. How often does he run?
 1. He runs on weekends.
 2. He runs on Saturday.
 3. He usually runs at 8:00.

Circle The Correct <u>Time</u> Reply:

A. When does he run?
   1. He often runs.
   2. He runs on Monday.
   3. He never runs.

B. When does she study?
   1. She studies on Tuesday.
   2. She studies always.
   3. She always studies.

C. When do they play?
   1. They always play.
   2. They seldom play.
   3. They play tomorrow.

D. When do you worry?
   1. We worry on Tuesday.
   2. We never worry.
   3. We weldom worry.

E. When do you travel?
   1. I never travel.
   2. I usually travel on Sunday.
   3. I travel on weekends.

Circle The Present <u>Continuous</u>:

A. He has breakfast.
   1. He breakfasts.
   2. He's having breakfast.
   3. He's breakfasting.

B. Time passes quickly.
   1. Time's passing quickly.
   2. Times pass quickly.
   3. Time is quickly

C. We have a game.
   1. We are a game.
   2. We are going to game.
   3. We're having a game.

D. We run together.
   1. We're running together.
   2. We're going to run together.
   3. We running together.

E. What do you say?
   1. What saying you?
   2. What are you saying?
   3. What do you saying?

Circle The Question:

A. It's getting late.
   1. It gets late?

B. It's time to get up.
   1. Is it time to get up?

2. Is it getting late?   2. Does it time to get up?

3. Is it late getting?   3. Has it time to get up?

C. Days run together.   D. I have plans for tomorrow.
  1. Have days run   1. Does he have plans tomorrow?
     together?   2. Has he plans for tomorrow?
  2. Do days run   3. Do you have plans for tomorrow
     together?
  3. Do run days
     together?

E. We can swim until noon.
  1. Can you swim until noon?
  2. Does we swim until noon?
  3. Has you swim until noon?

Circle Correct Meaning of Idiom:

A. She's a girl after my own   B. This is a clear cut lesson.
  heart.
  1. I like her.   1. We have to cut the les-
                                son.
  2. She has a heart.   2. The lesson is short cut.
  3. She has no heart.   3. This lesson is simple.

C. They study day in day out.   D. She says it time and again.
  1. They study during the day.   1. She says it many times.
  2. They always study.   2. She says it one time.
  3. They never study.   3. She says it once.

E. The weather's good all year.
  1. It's good every year.
  2. It's good the whole year.
  3. It's good once in a year.

Let's Converse
Chapter Three
Oral Comprehension - Sample Test

Teacher must explain that this test is oral in its entirety. Teacher will pronounce all sentences, student will only circle the correct replies. This test can also be used to evaluate student pronunciation by allowing individual student to pronounce the correct answer aloud.

I. Circle the correct <u>question</u>:

A. That's a book.
1. What's that?
2. What's this?
3. When's this?

B. It's a pencil.
1. What's that?
2. What's this?
3. Who's this?

C. They're coins.
1. What's that?
2. Who are they?
3. What are these?

D. I need a notebook.
1. What do you need?
2. What's this?
3. What's that?

E. We need pencils.
1. What's that?
2. do we need?
3. What's this?

F. You need a book.
1. Do I need a book?
2. Do they need a book?
3. Does he need a book?

G. They need supplies.
1. Does he need supplies?
2. Do they need supplies?
3. Does she need supplies?

H. Mary and Rodger need money.
1. Does they need money?
2. Does she need money?
3. Do they need money?

I. She needs a book.
1. Does he need a book?
2. Do they need a book?
3. Do we need a book?

J. The boy needs love.
1. Do the boys need love?
2. Does the boy need love?
3. Does she need love?

II. Circle the correct sentence with a <u>determiner</u>:

A. David reads at home.
1. He reads at home.

B. Mary reads at home.
1. They read at home.

2. She reads at home.
3. They read at home.

C. My Friend studies hard.
1. They study hard.
2. We study hard.
3. He studies hard.

E. Mary plays at school.
1. She plays at school.
2. They play at school.
3. We play at school.

2. She reads at home.
3. I read at home.

D. His teacher reads at home.
1. She reads at home.
2. He reads at home.
3. They read at home.

III. Circle the correct **negative**:

A. David at school.
1. David doesn't read at school.
2. David does read at school.
3. David do read at school.

B. We study at home.
1. We doesn't study at home.
2. We don't study at home.
3. They don't study at home.

C. She plays tennis.
1. They don't play tennis.
2. She don't play tennis.

3. She doesn't play tennis.

D. We eat breakfast.
1. We don't eat breakfast.
2. They don't eat breakfast.

3. She doesn't eat breakfast.

E. You write your lesson.
1. They don't write your lesson.
2. You don't write your lesson.
3. They doesn't write your lesson.

IV. Circle the correct **question**:

A. This book is one dollar.

1. How much is this book?

B. These rulers are two dollars.
1. How much is these rulers?

2. How much are these books? 2. how much are these rulers?
3. How much is these books? 3. How much is these rulers.

C. This notebook is 30 cents.
   1. How much are these notebooks?
   2. How much is these notebooks?
   3. How much is this notebook?

D. That ruler is 10 cents.
   1. How much is that ruler?
   2. How much is this ruler?
   3. How much are that ruler?

E. These books are 10 dollars.
   1. How much are this books?
   2. How much are these books?
   3. How much is these books?

V. Circle the correct question:

A. I need a book.
   1. What do you need?
   2. Where do you need?
   3. Why do you need?

B. I study in the classroom.
   1. What do you study?
   2. Where do you study?
   3. Why do you study?

C. He's my teacher.
   1. What's your teacher?

   2. Where's your teacher?
   3. Who's your teacher?

D. I eat at eight o'clock.
   1. What eats at eight o'clock'.
   2. When do you eat?
   3. Why do you eat?

E. I read because I must.
   1. When do you read?
   2. Who do you read?
   3. Why do you read?

ANSWERS TO TEST:

I. A. 1 B. 2 C. 3 D. 1 E. 2 F. 1 G. 2 H. 3 I. 1 J. 2
II. A. 1 B. 2 C. 3 D. 2 E. 1   III. A. 1 B. 2 C. 3 D. 1 E. 2
IV. A. 1 B. 2 C. 3 D. 1 E. 2   V. A. 1 B. 2 C. 3 D. 2 E. 3

Let's Converse

Chapter Five
Oral Comprehension—Sample Test

Teacher must explain that this test is oral in its entirety. Teacher will pronounce all sentences, student will only circle the correct replies. This test can also be used to evaluate student pronunciation by allowing individual student to pronounce the correct answer aloud.

I. Listen, then choose the correct reply:

A. Mrs. Browning comes to the doctor because
1. her daughter is sick.
2. she is sick.
3. both she and Lisa are sick.

B. Lisa knows she's sick, because
1. she feels well.
2. she has to study.
3. she didn't sleep all night.

C. Lisa is worried, because
1. She has to study.
2. her friends are coming to visit.
3. her mother has the flu.

D. The doctor gives Lisa
1. Medication.
2. something to read.
3. a new car.

E. Lisa went visiting in
1. her car.
2. her father's car.
3. her friend's car.

II. Circle the <u>past</u> <u>tense</u> of the sentence you hear:

A. I'm afraid.
1. I was afraid.
2. I'll be afraid.
3. I'm going to be afraid.

B. I feel sick.
1. I'll feel sick.
2. 1 felt sick.
3. 1 was feeling sick.

C. I can't sleep.
1. I wasn't sleeping.
2. I am not sleeping.
3. I couldn't sleep.

D. My eyes water.
1. My eyes watered.
2. My eyes have watered.
3. My eyes will water.

E. I sleep well.
   1. I have slept well.
   2. I slept well.
   3. I'll sleep well.

III. Circle the <u>question</u> of the sentence you hear:

A. He will be here at seven.
   1. Will he be here at seven?
   2. Will we be here at seven?
   3. Will they be here at seven?

B. Father will drive.
   1. Father will not drive.
   2. Will father drive?
   3. Won't father drive?

C. We will come soon.
   1. Will they come soon?
   2. Will she come soon?
   3. Will you come soon?

D. He will beat you.
   1. Will he beat you?
   2. Will she beat you?
   3. Will they beat you?

E. I'll see about that.
   1. Will they see about that?
   2. Will you see about that?
   3. Will she see about that?

IV. Circle the correct <u>question</u>:

A. It's my car.
   1. Whose car is this?
   2. Where's the car?
   3. What car is this?

B. This is his book.
   1. Where is his book?
   2. Whose book is this?
   3. What book is this?

C. This is my pencil.
   1. Where is my pencil?
   2. What's this pencil?
   3. Whose pencil is this?

D. This is your tea.
   1. Whose tea is this?
   2. Where's the tea?
   3. What's in the tea?

E. This is my rocket.
   1. Where is my rocket?
   2. Whose rocket is this?
   3. What's the rocket?

V. Circle the correct <u>reply</u>.

A. How does he read?
1. He reads easily.
2. He reads easy.
3. He easily reads.

B. How does she drive?
1. She carefully drives.
2. She drives carefully.
3. She drives careful.

C. How did he run?
1. He slowly ran.
2. He ran slow.
3. He ran slowly.

D. How did she sleep?
1. She slept restlessly.
2. She slept restless.
3. She restlessly slept.

E. How does he speak?
1. He speaks slow.
2. He slowly speaks.
3. He speaks slowly.

VI. Choose the correct <u>meaning</u>: When I say ... I mean:

A. He kept up his appearance.
1. He was well.
2. He was polite.
3. He seemed proper.

B. Lisa has the teacher's ear.
1. The teacher listens to Lisa
2. The teacher gave Lisa his ear.
3. Lisa likes the teacher's ear.

C . The little boy was hard headed.
1. He had a hard head.
2. He was stubborn.
3. His head hurt.

D. Mary shows promise in tennis.
1. Mary knows nothing about tennis
2. Mary knows little about tennis.
3. Mary is making progress in tennis

E. We talked Roger into playing.
1. We talked instead of playing.
2. He didn't want to, but we convinced him to play.
3. He didn't play.

ANSWERS TO TEST:

I. A. 1 B. 3 C. 2 D. I E. 2   II. A. I B. 2 C. 3 D. 1 E. 2
III.A. 1B. 2C. 3D. 1E.2   IV. A. 1 B. 2 C. 3 D. 1 E. 2
V. A. 1 B. 2 C. 3 D. 1 E. 3   VI. A. 3 B. 1 C. 2 D. 3 E. 2

Let's Converse
Sample Of Final Oral Comprehension Exam

I. Circle the correct <u>answer</u>:

A. Tom says
  1. it's hard finding work.
  2. it's hard to work.
  3. it's hard working.

B. Mary told Jim
  1. she got a job.
  2. Roger got a job.
  3. Tom got a job?

C. Roger got a job
  1. through Tom.
  2. through Mary.
  3. through an employment agency.

D. Roger isn't happy because
  1. he works.
  2. he hasn't been promoted.
  3. he wants a job.

E. Tom and Jim meet at
  1. the cafeteria.
  2. school.
  3. home.

II. Circle the correct <u>answer</u>:

A. Jack is so hungry, he
  1. could eat an elephant.
  2. could eat dinner.
  3. could eat a steak.

B. Jack prefers to eat
  1. in a cafeteria.
  2. in a restaurant.
  3. at home.

C. They must hurry to get there
  1. to eat
  2. before noon.

D. Jack will go out with Lisa
  1. to a restaurant.
  2. to a movie.

3. before the crowds.   3. to the river.

E. Lisa is coming to visit
  1. with Ed.
  2. for a weekend.
  3. with her mother.

III. Circle the correct <u>past</u> <u>tense</u>:

A. I'm afraid.
  1. I was afraid.
  2. I is afraid.
  3. I are afraid.

B. I don't try.
  1. I did tried.
  2. I didn't try.
  3. I do try.

C. My legs ache.
  1. My legs had ache.
  2. My legs do ache.
  3. My eyes have watered.

D. She tosses in bed.
  1. She tossed in bed.
  2. She does toss in bed.
  3. She toss in bed.

E. My eyes water.
  1. My eyes had water.
  2. My eyes watered.
  3. My eyes have watered.

iV. Circle the correct <u>response</u>:

A. How often does Mary come here?
  1. She rarely comes here.
  2. She rarely come here.
  3. She rare comes here.

B. How often do you play tennis?
  1. I hardly play tennis.
  2. I hardly ever play tennis.
  3. I play hard tennis.

C. How often do you have tests?
  1. I have test usual.
  2. I have test mostly.
  3. I seldom have tests.

D. Does he ever go on vacation?
  1. He frequent goes on vacation.
  2. He seldom goes on vacation.
  3. He goes not on

vacation.

E. How often do you have class?
1. I have class four times a week.
2. I have frequent class.
3. I have much class.

V. Circle the correct <u>pronoun</u>:

A. Does Lisa know Roger?
1. Yes, Lisa knows her.
2. Yes, Lisa knows him.
3. Yes, Lisa knows he.

B. Did she get the book?
1. Yes, she got it.
2. Yes, she got her.
3. Yes, she got him.

C. Do you know the Brownings?
1. Yes, we know him.
2. Yes, we know he.
3. Yes, we know them.

D. Did you see Tom last week?
1. Yes, I saw her.
2. Yes, I saw him.
3. Yes, I saw them.

E. Didn't he give you a racket?
1. No, he didn't give it to me.
2. No, he didn't give her to me.
3. No, he didn't give them to me.

VI. Circle the correct <u>reply</u>:

A. Is Jack good?
1. Jack is as good as Ed.
2. Jack is as better as Ed.
3. Jack is as better than Ed.

B. Does he write often?
1. He writes more often.
2. He writes as often as Mary.

3. He writes more often   .

    as Mary.

C. Did you eat a lot?
3. Yes, we ate as much as they did.

E. Is the meal complete?

1. Yes, we ate more as a lot.
2. Yes, we ate much as a lot.

D. Do you visit them often?
1. Yes, we visit them as often as we can.
2. Yes, we visit them more

often as we can.   3. Yes, we visit them
        much as we can.

1. Yes, the meal is more as complete.
2. Yes, the meal is as complete as yesterday's.
3. Yes, the meal is more complete as yesterday's.

ANSWERS TO TEST:
I. A. 1   B. 2   C. 3   D. 2   E. 1
II. A. 1   B. 2   C. 3   D. 1   E. 2
II. A. 1   B. 2   C. 3   D. 1   E. 2
IV. A. 1   B. 2   C. 3   D. 2   E. 1
V. A. 2   B. 1   C. 3   D. 2   E. 1
VI. A. 1   B. 2   C. 3   D. 1   E. 2

Let's Read: Chapter Two
Sample Test for *Reading Comprehension*

On the line, write another word with the same meaning as the word in *italics*.

_____ 1. The Campbells are a *usual* family.
_____ 2. Mr. Campbell is an *attorney*.
_____ 3. They *possess* a cabin in La Grange.
_____ 4. The cabin is *simple*.
_____ 5. They like visiting the *rural* area.
_____ 6. The beauty *compensates* for the discomfort.
_____ 7. They *purchase* groceries.
_____ 8. The children prepare for the *outing*.
_____ 9. They *assist* their Mother.
_____ 10. The Campbells *relax* at the picnic.

Fill in the word (phrase) most fitting to express the concept of the sentence according to the narrative.

A. Tim end Ann get up early Saturday to _____.
   1. go to school   2. help their father.
   3. drive to La Grange.   4. make sandwiches.

B. The Campbells stop on the highway to _____.
  1. stretch   2. study
  3. eat   4. read

C. People are always coming out to the river because _____.
  1. there are blankets   2. there are people
  3. there is a camping area   4. there is a trooper

D. Lucy is smiling and Mike knows _____.
  1. the boat will tip   2. Mother is waiting
  3. the falls are near   4. he can not be cross with he

E. Mike yells for help because _____.
  1. Lucy is not a good   2. he sees the trooper
     swimmer
  3. the falls are near   4. he sees his father

F. The two young Campbells are trembling because _____.
  1. they are dripping wet   2. they are at home
  3. they are under the blanket   4. they are afraid

G. Mrs. Campbell was worried _____.
  1. when Lucy and Mike   2. when the trooper came
     return
  3. when Lucy and Mike were   4. when Mr. Campbell yells
     late for supper

H. Before they go down far on the river _____.
  1. they must rent a canoe   2. they must tell Mrs. Campbell
  3. they must study the rapids   4. they must tell no one

I. Everyone is happy because _____.
  1. Mrs. Campbell is worried   2. Lucy and Mike are safe
  3. the trooper comes   4. the blanket is warm

J. Lucy is smiling as she _____.
  1. sits by the fire   3. rides the canoe
  2. talks to Ann   4. swims in the rapids

Place a check mark (✓) in front of the correct aanswer to each of the following questions according to the narrative.

1. Who are the Campbells?
___a. they are friends
___b. they are a typical American family
___c. they are smiling

3. Does Mrs. Campbell like being a housewife?
___a. yes, she does
___b. no, she doesn't
___c. she thinks about it

5. The Colorado River flows through
___a. the town
___b. the highway
___c. Houston

7. When do the Campbells go to La Grange?
___a. every day
___b. on Saturday and Sunday
___c. on Wednesday

9. Why must Lucy sit still?

___a. because she is smiling

___b. because the canoe will overturn
___c. because Mike is afraid

2. Who practices law?
___a. Mr. Campbell
___b. Mrs. Campbell
___c. Mike

4. How far is it to La Grange from Houston?
___a. two hundred miles
___b. one hundred five miles
___c. twenty five miles

6. Where are the rest areas?
___a. in Houston
___b. on the river
___c. on the highway

8. Why do people come out to the river?
___a. there are many people
___b. there is water
___c. there boats and canoes

10. How does the canoe tip over?
___a. the rapids carry it toward the falls
___b. Mike loses control
___c. Lucy is frightened

There are some statements listed below about the narrative. write T for *True* in front of each statment which you think is *True*. Write F for *False* if the statment is not *True*.

_____1. The Campbells are a typical American family.
_____2. Mr. Campbell practices law.
_____3. Mrs. Campbell likes her occupation.
_____4. The Campbells own a mansion in La Grange.
_____5. The countryside is flat in La Grange.
_____6. Their cabin is comfortable.
_____7. In La Grange the Campbells spend some weekends.
_____8. They get up late on Saturday.
_____9. Mike and Lucy usually help their father.
_____10. Mike is the youngest in the family.

Let's Read
Chapter Three—Sample Test

Below are some phrases taken from the narrative. Make complete sentences.

1. a	low	income
2. at	the	age
3. the	second	oldest
4. in	the	family
5. from	the	other side
6. where	he	lived
7. in	deep	trouble
8. to	seek	counsel
9. of	Mike	Campbell
10. when	the	busing

Substitute the *Synonym* for the word underlined.

1. Curtis was in deep <u>trouble</u>.

2. They <u>offered</u> equal opportunity.

3. Mr. Campbell <u>listened</u> attentively.

4. It was his <u>constitutional</u> right.

5. The <u>guards</u> accused Curtis.

6. The judge was <u>confused</u>.

7. A thorough <u>investigation</u> was ordered.

8. They did not treat him as an <u>equal</u>.

9. Curtis wanted to <u>contribute</u>.

10. The judge was not <u>stern</u>.

Each space may be filled by a word or phrase. Where possible, use variations of the missing words.

Mr. Campbell _____ attentively. He _____ many notes. He was going to _____ them in _____. They _____ Curtis to _____. It was his _____ right.

The guards _____ accusing _____. They _____ that Curtis _____ into the warehouse. The judge _____ his gavel. The neighbors _____ his innocence. They _____ he was a _____ boy.

The judge was _____. A man must be _____ beyond _____ doubt. He can _____ be convicted _____. The _____ _____ of a plan. A _____ investigation was _____.

Circle the word most like (Column II), and most unlike (Column III), the phrase in Column I.

COLUMN I	COLUMN II	COLUMN III
1. able	a. adequate b. spacious c. clean	a. least b. unable c. inexpensive
2. accept	a. equal b. see c. approve	a. reject b. look c. meet
3. attend	a. call b. be present c. advise	a. dispatch b. deter c. be absent

4. benefit
    a. profit   a. care
    b. work   b. lose
    c. complete   c. earn

5. confused
    a. perplexed a. near
    b. glad   b. reasonable
    c. happy   c. orderly

6. deep
    a. spacious   a. congested
    b. profound   b. shallow
    c. least   c. most

7. follow
    a. succeed   a. cover up
    b. reveal   b. avoid
    c. disclose   c. precede

8. philanthropist
    a. well-bred person a. misanthrope
    b. clean person   b. lower class person
    c. humanitarian   c. dirty person

9. sentence
    a. judgment   a. condemnation
    b. suspension b. story
    c. trust   c. dismissal

10. somebody
    a. something   a. nobody
    b. sentry   b. anything
    c. someone   c. nothing

In the Space on the left write the word(s) which best fit the expression <u>underlined</u>.

_____ 1. Curtis Smith was a <u>humanitarian</u>.
_____ 2. Curtis came from the <u>lower class</u>.
_____ 3. But it wasn't <u>dirty</u>.
_____ 4. Curtis was in <u>profound</u> trouble.
_____ 5. Mr. Campbell gave his <u>advice</u>.
_____ 6. They <u>gave</u> him equal education.
_____ 7. Curtis was a member of a <u>group</u>.
_____ 8. The judge <u>heard</u> the witnesses.
_____ 9. The witnesses were <u>sympathetic</u>.
_____ 10. This was Curtis's <u>inherent</u> right.

Let's Read: Chapter Four
Sample Test for *Reading Comprehension*

Read the following sentences. Repeat, substituting, where possible, the synonym of the word underlined, or a phrase which explains the meaning. Make other necessary changes.

Example: She was an <u>extraordinary</u> woman.

           She was a remarkable woman.

1. Because of their <u>cruelty</u>, she was in custody.

_____

2. They made it <u>clear</u> in a newspaper article.

_____

3. The child was <u>agitated</u>.

_____

4. Signs of abuse were <u>evident</u>.

_____

5. She was <u>reluctant</u> to stay.

_____

6. Lori always <u>returned</u> home.

_____

7. Her <u>capacity</u> to feel was extraordinary.

_____

8. She doesn't know about her <u>illness</u>.

_____

9. Mrs. Campbell knew Lori's health was <u>terminal</u>.

_____

10. The Campbell children <u>remained</u> helpful.

_____

Fill in the blanks with words from the narrative. Each space may be filled by a word or phrase. Do not refer back to the narrative. Where possible, use variations of the missing words.

     Signs _____ abuse were _____. Lori's _____ were different. She _____ more mature _____ most children eight years _____ age. Her eyes had a _____ sadness _____ them. Lori was _____ _____ stay _____ two foster homes.

     Even though Lori was _____ _____ home, she always _____ there. The capacity _____ feel Lori is _____," said the _____ worker. Mrs. Campbell said,

"We'll do _____ we can _____ her when she _____ us."

In the space on the left write the word(s) which would best fit the expression underlined. Make other necessary changes.

    _____1. Lori came to the <u>adoptive</u> agency.
    _____2. Signs of <u>improper</u> <u>treatment</u> were evident.
    _____3. Her parents were <u>cruel</u>.
    _____4. Lori was under <u>agitated</u> neglect.
    _____5. She was <u>reluctant</u> to stay in foster homes.
    _____6. Lori's <u>customs</u> were different.
    _____7. She seemed more <u>ripe</u> than other children.
    _____8. She looked <u>depressed</u>.
    _____9. <u>Prior</u> to that she stayed in two foster homes.
    _____10. They increased her emotional <u>doubts</u>.

Place a check mark (✓) in front of the correct answer to each of the question according to the narrative.

1. Lori was in custody of the agency because
    ____a. she was a child of eleven
    ____b. of the cruelty of her parents
    ____c. she liked her sister
2. A newspaper article made it known that
    ____a. Lori was up for adoption
    ____b. Lori was ill
    ____c. Lori was at the Campbells

3. Mrs. Campbell learned about Lori from
    ____a. her neighbors
    ____b. the agency
    ____c. the newspaper

4. Lori's manners were different because
    ____a. she was a girl
    ____b. she seemed more mature
    ____c. she was depressed
   5. Lori returned to her home
    ____a. to see her mother

_____b. to run away

_____c. to help her little sister and brother

Below there are three (3) different thoughts expressed in each of the exercises. assign the proper sequence (Order) of thought according to the narrative.

1. a. in a newspaper article   _____
   b. the agency made it known   _____
   c. that Lori was up for adoption   _____
2. a. in custody of the agency   _____
   b. of her parents, she was   _____
   c. because of the cruelty   _____
3. a. and asked to see Lori   _____
   b. the welfare agency   _____
   c. she called   _____
4. a. speak to the agent about her   _____
   b. the first time she saw Lori   _____
   c. Mrs. Campbell knew she had better   _____
5. a. eight years of age   _____
   b. mature than most children   _____
   c. she seemed more   _____

Let's Read: Final Evaluation
Sample Test
The Would-be President

1. Mike has never been this excited before. He came home from school earlier than usual. "Mom!" he yelled. "I'm running for student council!" Mrs. Campbell sensed something unusual in her son's behavior. "Let's have a cola, Mike," she suggested, and you can tell me all about it."

They sat at the table. Mike told her that he has been asked by the student council president to run. "I think they had a wide choice of candidates. But they selected me. They think I'll surely win."

"I'm glad they want you, Mike. But don't be too sure of yourself," Mrs. Campbell cautioned.

"There are four other candidates, but I'm sure I have a good chance to win," Mike repeated. He was excited.

Read the following sentences. substitute where possible the synonym of the word <u>underlinded</u>, or a phrase that explains the meaning. Make other necessary changes.

1. We will proceed with <u>care</u>.
2. You won't hear any <u>noise</u>.
3. Mike was really <u>concerned</u>.
4. You'll say it <u>forcefully</u>.
5. Mrs. Campbell <u>proudly</u> listened to Mike's words.

Select one of three (3) words (Phrases) that best fulfills the meaning of the sentences according to the narrative. Insert the word in the blank space.

1. Mike was excited because he was _____ for president of the student body.
   a. running   b. voting   c. unusual

2. The student council had a wide choice of candidates, but they _____ Mike.
   a. told   b. selected   c. repeated

3. Mike was sure of winning, but Mrs. Campbell _____ him.
   a. excited   b. selected   c. cautioned

4. When he ran for president, Mike was constantly _____.
   a. on a merry-go-round   b. excited   c. slow

5. Mike could not _____ because things _____ fast.
   a. slow down,   b. understand it,   c. rest well,
      progressed   got   went

There are some statements listed below about the narrative. write

T for *True* in front of each statement that you think is <u>True</u>. write
F for <u>False</u> if the statemetn is not *True*.

_____ 1. Mike was going to rest when he won.
_____ 2. Mike's dressing habits changed.
_____ 3. The Campbells listened to Mike's speech.
_____ 4. Mrs. Campbell didn't encourage her son.
_____ 5. It was easy for Mike to prepare his speech.
_____ 6. Mike said that there must be many requests.

THE ENCHANTED MOUNTAIN

"I wish to leave this place right now !" Lucy cried. "I want to go home to my family. Please, let me go! You are more cruel than anyone I know. Even Miss Conklin, the history teacher!" At the first sight of tears, even quicker than you could say "Erutuf," the little creatures were all gone. The bathers were gone too. Only Lucy was left, her eyes closed, alone and no longer frightened.

When she opened her eyes, she was with her family. There was a look of concern in her parents' faces. Lucy sensed that something had happened. She knew that she would have to explain. Grown-ups always want things explained. But as hard as she tried, Lucy was unable to explain. She decided then it would be better to draw a picture. Someday, she would do this, not just now.

Read the following sentences. substitute where possible, the synonym of the word <u>underlinded</u>, or a phrase that explains the meaning. Make other necessary changes.

1. She was out of <u>peril</u>.
2. There was a look of <u>concern</u>.
3. Lucy <u>sensed</u> that something had happened.
4. She had to explain the <u>unfamiliar</u> place.
5. Lucy was <u>unable</u> to do it.
6. She had been <u>astonished</u>.

In the space on the left write the word(s) that best fit the expression <u>underlined</u>. Make other necessary changes.

1. They were punished for being <u>avaricious</u>.
2. We detest <u>water</u>.
3. How could anyone be <u>biased</u> here?
4. You'll be <u>astonished</u> to hear this.
5. We do very <u>uncomplicated</u> things here.
6. She replied <u>promptly</u>.

Fill in the most appropriate word (Phrase) to express the <u>concept</u> of the sentences according to the narrative.

1. Those Erutuf who bathed in the lake were being _____.
   1. rewarded   2. chastised   3. loved   4. hated

2. Lucy was silent because she didn't want to _____ the little creature.
   1. investigate   2. conjecture   3. hurt   4. love

3. Lucy didn't understand how anyone could be _____ on the mountain.
   1. prejudiced   2. hated   3. loved   4. astonished

4. Lucy wanted to return now because she thought that the Erutuf were _____.
   1. prejudiced   2. cruel   3. biased   4. quiet

5. Lucy knew she would have to _____ because grown-ups want things _____.

1. explain,	2. hate,	3. stand,	4. punish,
explained	loved	simple	rewarded

There are some statements listed below about the narrative. Write <u>T</u> for *True* in front of each statement that you think is *True*. Write <u>F</u> for *False* if the statement is not *True*.

_____ 1. Lucy was afraid to hurt the little creature's feelings.
_____ 2. The Erutuf people do simple things.

_____ 3. The incorrigibles were punished more severely than mere repeaters.

_____ 4. The incorrigibles became colorless and shapeless.

_____ 5. The incorrigibles were given good food.

_____ 6. When Lucy cried, the Erutuf people disappeared.

Let's Write
Chapter One—Sample Test

In the spaces provided on the right, write examples of words which use the prefix.

LATIN ORIGIN
Example: ante — before, in front — antecede, antecedent,
antedate

PREFIX	AREA OF MEANING	EXAMPLES
ab-	away from	
bene-	well	
contra-	against, opposite	
dis-	apart, away, not (negative)	
mal-	ill, bad, badly	

In the space provided on the right, write examples of words which use the prefix.

GREEK ORIGIN
Example: arch — chief, primitive, the earlier — archaic

In the space provided on the right, write examples of words which use the prefix.

ANGLO-SAXON ORIGIN
Example: a — at, in, on, to — ahead, afoot, asleep

Change Verbs into Nouns. Follow the examples.

	VERB	NOUN
EXAMPLE:	refuse	refusal
1.	propose	_____
2.	survive	_____
3.	approve	_____
4.	dismiss	_____
EXAMPLE:	examine	examination

5.	recognize	_____
6.	denounce	_____
7.	realize	_____
8.	emigrate	_____
9.	define	_____

EXAMPLE:	develop	<u>development</u>
10.	pay	_____
11.	argue	_____
12.	invest	_____
13.	agree	_____
14.	punish	_____

Summary of Parts of Speech. Fill in the missing form of the word. Follow the example on top of the table.

NOUN	VERB	ADJECTIVE	ADVERB
economy	economize	economical	economically
	dramatize		
		hopeful	
			memorably
reversal			

Analyzing Words. Write your analysis on the lines provided.

1. <u>amare</u>

(a) What is an <u>amorous</u> person?

_____

(b) What is meant by the word <u>enamor</u>?

_____

(c) How is the word amateur related to <u>amare</u>?

_____

(d) Is the word amiable related to <u>amare</u>?

_____

2. <u>logos</u> -- <u>bios</u>

(a) What do we mean by saying "<u>He</u> <u>is</u> <u>logical</u>?"

(b) What does <u>biology</u> literally mean?

(c) Combine another root with <u>logos</u> and explain the meaning.

(d) Combine another root with <u>bios</u> and explain the meaning.

3. <u>anthropos</u> -- <u>logos</u>

(a) What is the literal meaning of <u>anthropology</u>?

(b)

(c)

(d) What is another word for <u>misanthropy</u>?

4. <u>mal-</u>

(a) What is the meaning of the word <u>malfunction</u>?

(b) How is malevolent related to the prefix <u>mal-</u>?

(c) Which other word(s) will express <u>maltreat</u>?

(d) What is the relation of <u>mal-</u> to <u>mis-</u>?

5. <u>fortis</u>

(a) What does <u>fortify</u> mean?

(b) What does <u>fortitude</u> mean?

(c) Is comfort related to <u>fortis</u>?

(d) What is a <u>fort</u>?

_____

Let's Write
Chapter Four—Sample Test

Select the word (Phrase) from the following list that best completes each of the sentences below. You may use one word more than once.

Example: We are <u>puzzled</u> about love.
         Love is <u>mysterious</u>.

good	origin	unselfish	assurance	become
changes	deception	lasting	strong	natural

1. We hold a <u>special</u> <u>affection</u> for nature. It is _____ for man to love his environment.

2. Man may have <u>come</u> <u>from</u> the water. Water may have been man's _____.

3. Parents <u>care</u> <u>more</u> <u>for</u> <u>their</u> <u>children</u> <u>than</u> for themselves. They are _____.

4. True love is not a sensation to be <u>soon</u> <u>forgotten</u>. It is a _____ relationship.

5. Giving in love aims at <u>pleasing</u> <u>the</u> <u>other</u> <u>person</u>. This giving is truly _____.

Correct the following sentences for <u>Dangling</u> <u>Modifiers</u>. Write the corrected sentence in the space provided.

Example: Walking into the hall, the air felt cooler.
<u>Walking into the hall, she felt the air grow cooler.</u>

6. Singing a song, the place was much happier. _____

_____

7. Reaching maturity, my mother allowed me to go out on a date.

8. Spending a week in the mountains, the home was more enjoyable,

9. Realizing the need for each other, the house was filled with love.

10. Looking out of the window, the landscape was beautiful.

Use the <u>Opposites</u> to rewrite the following sentences. Make any necessary changes to suit the new sentences.

Example: question - answer
We ask a <u>question</u>.
We give an <u>answer</u>.

appear	strong	uncivilized	same	together
sick	unselfish	sad	comfort	natural

11. Love brings on <u>different</u> feelings.

12. We live in a <u>civilized</u> world.

13. My heart is <u>glad</u>.

14. Love means being your <u>unnatural</u> self.

15. Where there is no love, fear and deception <u>vanish</u>.

16. The love between man and woman is <u>weak</u>.

17. The giving in love is <u>selfish</u>.

18. <u>Healthy</u> persons can become well again.

19. They find <u>discomfort</u> in the touch of a hand.

20. Love can bring <u>apart</u> people of different ages.

Answer each of the following questions with a complete sentence.

Example: What are we puzzled about?
<u>We're puzzled about love.</u>

21. How do children regard love?

_____

22. Why does love change constantly?

_____

23. What do we hold for nature?

_____

24. Why does man go back to water?

_____

25. What are the basic needs?

_____

Commentary on Model

26. Tell what you learned about <u>true</u> <u>love</u> from section 4.

Let's Write
Chapter Five—Sample Test

From the list of words preceding each section fill each blank space. you may use a word more than once. Also, you may use more than one word in one blank space.

| sibling | traffic | car | father | space |
| school | days | block | children | place |

Mr. Axby waits in the _____ while his _____ come out of _____. This happens only on _____ when it rains. At times there is too much _____ and Mr. Axby can not find a to park. When this happens, he drives many times around the _____. The _____ are worried, but their

_____ arrives as soon as the _____ is available.

at   to the cemetery   miss

at the	stand	usually
remember	happy	while
cheerful	resourceful	grave
after	recall	nowadays
always	graveside	cherish
every	memories	long

_____ year the Axbys go _____ _____ _____ and place flowers on Mrs. Axby's _____. _____ they stand _____ _____ graveside, they _____ the good times. Mrs. Axby always told them to _____ her and reminded them to be _____. _____ they _____ her _____ personality. She was _____ and _____ . The day _____ ends with a long hike _____ they leave for home. The Axbys remember and _____ their _____ .

Make the necessary change(s) when you substitute the new element into your sentence.

Example: The Axbys live on Shadywood street. (Ralph)
Ralph lives on Shadywood street.

1. The <u>siblings</u> go to the neighborhood school. (Dorothy)
2. Mr. Axby has <u>three</u> children. (one)
3. <u>He</u> <u>attends</u> Meridian High. (They)
4. <u>He</u> does well in school. (We)
5. <u>John</u> loves to study and to read. (I)
6. <u>She</u> loves studying but not reading. (They)
7. <u>She</u> is in a habit of reading rapidly. (I)
8. <u>Dorothy</u> was ill all of last week. (We)
9. <u>She</u> is doing some chores around the house. (Ralph and Susan)
10. <u>She</u> vacumms her room. (They)

Let's Write
Chapter Seven—Sample Test

Select <u>Two</u> topics below and write one paragraph on each. Remember to include an introductory (Topic) sentence within the

paragraph itself. Follow the <u>Topic</u> <u>Sentence</u> with a <u>Body</u> and the <u>Concluding</u> statement

1. How to change a car tire.
2. How to climb a mountain.
3. How to say "good night" to a date.
4. Description of the person you love.
5. Description of a flower.

Let's Continue
Chapter Six—Sample Test

Complete the sentences below. Use the correct modal auxiliary: can, may, must, should, shall. Then write one additional sentence using the modal from the example. Read all of the sentences aloud.

1. Express <u>ability</u>
   a. Sue _____ drive well.

   _____

   b. I _____ stop on time.

   _____

   c. Some people _____ not concentrate.

   _____

   d. When _____ you come to see me?

   _____

   e. _____ you go out with us tonight?

   _____

   f. No, I _____. Sue is feeling bad.

   _____

2. Express <u>necessity</u>
   a. I _____ be at the office by 9:30 a.m..

   _____

   b. _____ you always interrupt me?

   _____

   c. We _____ all observe traffic laws.

   _____

d. I _____ confess. Yesterday I got a ticket, too.

_____

e. You _____ laugh at Sue for getting a ticket.

_____

3. Express <u>advisability</u> or <u>obligation</u>.
   a. I _____ laugh at Sue, because I got a ticket, too.

   _____

   b. You _____ know better, Glenn. There are traffic
   signs all over. _____

   _____

   c. The police don't tell you where the speed traps are. I don't
      think they _____.

   _____

   d. Traffic tickets are commonplace. But I really _____
      have gotten one.

   _____

   e. You _____ always slow down.

   _____

4. Express <u>permission</u>.
   a. _____ I borrow your car? No, you _____ not.

   _____

   b. _____ Rhonda spend the night? Yes, she _____.

   _____

   c. Try to forget it. I _____ just do that.

   _____

   d. _____ I use the bathroom? Yes, you _____.

   _____

   e. Francis have a drink of water?

   _____

5. Express <u>possibility</u>.
   a. I'm afraid something _____ go wrong.

   _____

   b. It _____ or _____ not snow tomorrow.

FIVE WEEKS OF ELEMENTARY
ENGLISH AS A SECOND LANGUAGE
SYLLABUS

TEXT: *Phase Zero Plus: Let's Begin.*

Week	Chapter	Exercises	Lab
1	Getting Started p. 1 through 14 (ONE)	1, 2, 3, 4, 5, 6, 7, 8, 9, 10, 11, 12, 13, 14	
	p. 15, 16, 17, 18, 19, 20	p. 17, 20	p. 21, 22
	p. 22, 23, 24, 25, 26,	p, 26, 27, 28, 29	
	p. 29, 30 p. 35, 36	p. 30, 31, 32, 33, 34, 35	
	(TWO)		
2	p. 37, 38, 40, 41, 42	p. 39, 43	p. 38, 39
	p. 45, 46, 47, 48, 49, 50, 51, 52, 56, 57	p. 52, 53, 54, 55	p. 43, 44, 45
		p. 57 (Writing)	
	p. 58	38 (Dialogue)	

Week	Chapter in Class	Exercises (at Home)	Lab
	(THREE)		
2 (continued)	p. 59, 60, 64, 65, 66, 67, 69, 70, 71 p. 72, 73, 74, 75 p. 79, 80, 81, 83, 84	p. 61-p. 68, 69 71, 72 (Copy) p. 76 (Copy)- p. 77, 78, 79, 81, 82, 83	p. 60, 61 62, 63 64
3	**(FOUR)**		
	p. 85, 86, 87, 88, 89 90, 91, 93, 94, 95 p. 96, 98, 99, 101 (Listen & Write)101	p. 88 (Copy), 91 (Copy) 95, 96 (Copy) 97 p. 100, 101, 102, 103, 104, 105 p. 108, 109, 110, 111, 112	p. 92
	(FIVE)		
	p. 113, 114 116, 117, 118, 119, 122, 124, 125 (Describe drawings), p. 125, 126, 127 (Answer) p. 128, 129, 130	P. 115, 116 (Copy)119 (Copy)127 (Copy) p.131, 132, 133	p. 114, 115, 116, 118, 119 p.120, 121

Week	Chapter in Class	Exercises (at Home)	Lab
3 (continued)	p. 133, 134, 135, 136, 137, 138		
	p. 138 (Listen & Write)	p. 139, 140, 141,	
	p. 141 (Repeat), 142	p. 143, 144, 145, 146	
	p. 146 (Uncramble)	p. 147, 148	
	(SIX)		
	p. 149, 150-p. 151 (Listen & Write) 152, 153	p. 151 (Copy)	p.150
	p. 154, 155 (Listen & Write) p. 158, 159, 160 162, 163, 164, 168, 169	p. 155 (Copy) p. 157, 158, 161,162	p. 156, 157
	p. 170, 171, 172	p. 164, 165, 166, 167- 170, 173, 174	p.168
4	(SEVEN)		
	p. 175, 176, 178, 179,180, 181 183, 184,185, 186, 187, 188, 189, 190, 191,		p. 176, 177 p. 181, 182, 183, 188 p. 193

Week	Chapter in Class	Exercises (at Home)	Lab
4 (continued)	192, 193, 194, 195, 196, 197, 198, 199, & 200	178 (Copy)-p. 181-2 (Copy)-p. 185, 186, 187 (Write) 189 (Copy) 191 (Write) 201, 202, 203, 204, 205, 206	
	(EIGHT)		
	p. 207, 208, 210, 211,212, 213, 214, 216, 217, 218, 219, 220, 221, p. 224, 227, 228, 229	210 (Copy), 214 (Copy) p. 221, 222. 223, 224, 225, 226, 230, 231	209-p. 214 215, 216, 218
5	(NINE)		
	p. 233, 234, 236, 237, 238, 242, 247 (Review), 248, 249, 250, 251, 252,253, 254, 225, 226, 227, 228, 229, 260	p. 235, 236 (Copy) p. 243, 244. 245. 246, 247, 248, 249, 256, 257, 258, 259	p. 234, 238, 239, 240, 241 243, 255
	(TEN)		
	p. 261, 262, 265. 266, 267, 270, 271, 272, 275, 276, 277, 285 286, 288	p. 264 (Copy)- p. 267 (Copy)- p. 272, 273, 274 p. 278, 279, 280, 281, 282, 283,284, 287	p.263, 266, 268, 269, 270, 277

FALL OR SPRING SEMESTER ELEMENTARY ENGLISH AS A SECOND LANGUAGE

SYLLABUS

TEXT: *Phase Zero Plus: Let's Begin.*

Week	Chapter in Class	Exercises (at Home)	Lab
1 - 4	Getting Started p. 1 through 14	p. 1, 2, 3, 4, 5, 6, 7, 8, 9, 10, 11, 12, 13, 14	
	(ONE)		
	p. 15, 16, 17, 18, 19, 20, 22, 23, 24, 25, 26, 29, 30,35, 36	p. 17, 20 p. 21, 27, 28, 29 p. 30, 31, 32, 33, 34, 35	p. 21-22
	(TWO)		
	p, 37, 38, 40, 41, 42 p. 45, 46, 47, 48, 49, 50, 51, 52, 56, 57, 58	p. 39, 43 p. 52, 53, 54, 55 p. 57 (Writing) 38 (Dialogue)	p. 38, 39 p. 43, 44, 45

Week	Chapter in Class	Exercises (at Home)	Lab
	(THREE)		
5-7	p.59, 60, 64, 65, 67, 69, 70, 71, 71, 72, (Copy) 62, 63	p 61, 68, 69, p. 60, 61, 71, 72 (Copy) 62, 63	p. 60, 61, 62, 63 64
	p. 72, 73, 74, 75, 79, 80, 81, 83, 84	p.76 (Copy) 77, 78, 79, 81, 82, 83	
	(FOUR)		
	p. 85, 86, 87, 88, 89, 90, 91, 93, 94, 95	p. 88 (Copy) 91 (Copy) p. 95, 96 (Copy) 97,	p. 92
	p. 96, 98, 99, 101 (Listen & Write) 105-7	p. 100, 101, 102, 103, 104, 105 p. 108, 109, 110, 111, 112	
	(FIVE)		
	p. 113, 114, 116, 117, 118, 119, 122, 124, 125 (Describe drawings),	p. 115, 116 (Copy) p.119 (Copy) 127 (Copy)	p. 114, 115, 116, 117, 118, 119 p.120, 121
	p. 125, 126, 127 (Answer) p. 128, 129, 130	p.131, 132, 133	

Week	Chapter in Class	Exercises (at Home)	Lab
	p. 133, 134, 135, 136, 137, 138		
	p. 138 (Listen & Write)	p. 139, 140, 141-	
	p. 141 (Repeat), 142	p. 143, 144, 145, 146	
	p. 146 (Unscramble)	p. 147, 148	
	(SIX)		
8-10	p. 149, 151, (Listen & Write) 152, 153	p.151 (Copy)	p. 150
	p. 154, 155 (Listen & Write)	p.155 (Copy)-	p. 156, 157
	p. 158, 159, 160-p. 162, 163, 164-p. 168, 169	p. 157, 158 161, 162, 164, 165, 166, 167-	
	p. 170, 171, 172	170 173, 174	p.168
	(SEVEN)		
	p. 175, 176, 178, 179, 180, 181-p.183, 184, 185, 186, 187, 188, 189, 190, 191, 192, 193, 194, 195, 196, 197, 198, 199 & 200	p. 178 (Copy)- p.181-2 (Copy) 185- p. 187 (Write)- p.189 (Copy)- p.191 (Write) p.201, 202, 203, 204, 205, 206	p. 176, 177 p. 181, 182, 183,-p. 188 p. 193

Week	Chapter in Class	Exercises (at Home)	Lab
	(EIGHT)		
11-12	p. 207, 208-p.210, 211, 212, 213, 214, 216, 217, 218, 219, 220, 221- p. 224, 227, 228, 229	p. 210 (Copy)-p.214 (Copy) p. 221, 222, 223, 224, 225, 226, 230, 231	p. 209, 214, 215, 216 p. 218
	(NINE)		
	p. 233, 234-p.236, 237, 238, 242 p. 247 (Review), 248, 249, 250, 251, 252, 253, 254, 255-260	p. 235, 236 (Copy) p. 243, 244, 245, 246, 247, 248, 249- p. 256, 257, 258, 259	p. 234-p. 238, 239, 240, 241-243-p.255
	(TEN)		
13-14	p. 261, 262-p.265, 266, 267, 270, 271, 272, 275, 276, 277, 285, 286-p.288	p. 264 (Copy)-p. 267 (Copy)-p. 272, 273, 274 p. 278, 279, 280	p. 263, 264, 266, 267, 270, 271, 277, 278
15	Comprehensive Reviewing & Final Evaluation		

FIVE WEEKS
SUMMER SYLLABUS
FOR INTERMEDIATE CONVERSATION

TEXT: *Phase One: Let's Converse.*

Week	Chapter in Class	Exercises (at Home)
	Introduction	
	(ONE)	
1	p. 1, Episodes 1, 2	p. 2, Drawing & Dialogues
	p. 3, Episodes 3, 4 p.	p. 3, 4, Drawings & Dialogue
	4, Words & Questions p.	p. 7, 8, 9
	5, 6, 7, Pronunciation Drill	p. 14, 15, 16, 17
	p. 10, 11, 12, 13, 14	
	p. 18, 19 Idioms	
	(TWO)	
	p. 21, Episodes 1, 2	p. 22, Drawings & Dialogues
	p. 23, Episode 3	p. 24, Drawing & Dialogue
	p. 24, Episode 4	p. 27, Phrases, p. 28, Sentences
	p. 24, Bonus Dialogue	p. 30, Vocabulary
	p. 25, Words & Questions	p. 37, 38, 39, 40, 41
	p. 26, 27, Pronunciation Drill	
	p. 29, Statements	
	p. 31, 32, 33, 34, 35, 36	
	p. 41, Idioms	

Week	Chapter in Class	Exercises (at Home)
	(THREE)	
2	p. 43, Episodes 1, 2 p. 45, Episodes 3, 4 p. 46, Episode 5 p. 47, 48, 49 p. 51, 52, 53, 54, 55 p. 56, 57, 58, 59, 60, 61, 62 p. 68, Idioms	p. 44, Drawings & Dialogues p. 108, Vocabulary p. 118, 119, 120, 121, 122, 123, 124, 125
	(FOUR)	
	p. 71, Episodes 1, 2 p. 72, Episodes 3, 4 p. 74, 75 p. 77, 78, 79, 80 p. 82, 83, 84, 85 p. 88, 89 - p. 94, Idioms & Traffic Signs	p. 72, Drawing & Dialogue p. 73, Drawing & Dialogue p. 73-4 Words & Questions p. 76, A & B p. 77, Sentences p. 81, Vocabulary & Numbers p. 86, 87 p. 90, 91, 92, 93
	(FIVE)	
3	p. 97-8, Episodes 1, 2 p. 98, 99, Episodes 3, 4 p. 99, Episode 5 p. 101, 102, 103 p. 104, 105, 106, 107 p. 109, 110, 111, 112, 113, 114, 115, 116, 117 p. 126, 127, 128, 129 p. 130, 131, Idioms & Poems	p. 98, Drawing & Dialogue p. 100, Drawing & Dialogue p. 100-1 Words & Questions p. 103, A & B p. 104, Sentences p. 108, Vocabulary p. 118, 119, 120, 121, 122, 123, 124, 125

Week	Chapter in Class	Exercises (at Home)
	(SIX)	
	p. 133-4, Episodes 1, 2 p. 134-5, Episodes 3, 4 p. 136-8, Pronunciation p. 140, 141, 142, 143, 144 p. 145, 146, 147, 148, 149 p. 150, 151, 152, 153, 154, 155 p. 160, 161, Idioms	p. 134 Drawing & Dialogue p. 135, Drawing & Dialogue p. 136, Words & Questions p. 138-9, A & B - p. 139-40, Sentences p. 144, Vocabulary A & B p. 155, 156, 157, 158, 159
	(SEVEN)	
4	p. 163-4, Episodes 1, 2 p. 164-5, Episodes 3, 4, 5 p. 167, 168 p. 170, 171, 172, 173, 174, 175, 176, 177 p. 178, 179, 180, 181, 182, 183, 184, 185, 186, 187 p. 193, Idioms	p. 164, Drawing & Dialogue p. 166, Drawing & Dialogue Words & Questions p. 168, A, p. 169, B, p. 169-70, Sentences p. 177, Vocabulary p. 187, 188, 189, 190, 191, 192, 193
	(EIGHT)	
	p. 195-6, Episodes 1, 2 196-7 Episodes 3, 4 p. 198, 199, 200 p. 202, 203 p. 204, 205, 206, 207, 208, 209, 210, 211, 212, 213, 214, 215 p. 222, Idioms, p. 223	p. 196, Drawing & Dialogue p. 197, Drawing & Dialogue p. 198, Words & Questions p. 200, A - p. 201-2, B & Sentences p. 203-4, Vocabulary p. 215, 216, 217, 218, 219, 220, 221, 222

Week	Chapter in Class	Exercises (at Home)
	(NINE)	
5	p. 225, 226, Episodes 1, 2 p. 226, 227, Episodes 3, 4 p. 228, 229, Episodes 5, 6 p. 230, 231, 232 p. 234, 235, 236, 237, 238, 239, 240, 241, 242, 243, 244, 245, 246 p. 254 Idioms	p. 226, Drawing & Dialogue p. 227, Drawing & Dialogue p. 228, Drawing & Dialogue p. 229, Words & Questions p. 232, A & B, p. 233, Sentences p. 246, 247, 248, 289, 250, 251, 252, 253, 254
	(TEN)	
	p. 257-8, Episodes 1, 2 p. 258-9, Episode 3 p. 259, 260, 261, 262 p. 263, 264, 265, 266 p. 268, 269, 270, 271, 272, 273, 274 p. 279, Idioms	p. 258, Drawing & Dialogue p. 259, Drawing & Dialogue p. 262, Words & Questions p. 266, A, p. 267-8, B, Sentences p. 274, 275, 276, 277, 278, 279

FALL OR SPRING SEMESTER SYLLABUS FOR INTERMEDIATE CONVERSATION

Text: *Phase One: Let's Converse*

Week	Chapter in Class	Exercises (at Home)
	Introduction	
	(ONE)	
1-4	p. 1, Episodes 1, 2	p. 2, Drawings & Dialogues
	p. 3, Episodes 3, 4	p. 3, 4, Drawings & Dialogues
	p. 4, Words & Questions	p. 7, 8, 9
	p. 5, 6, 7, Pronunciation Drill	p. 14, 15, 16, 17
	p. 10, 11, 12, 13, 14	
	p. 18, 19 Idioms	
	(TWO)	
	p. 21, Episodes 1, 2	p. 22, Drawings & Dialogues
	p. 23, Episode 3	
	p. 24, Episode 4	p. 24, Drawing & Dialogue
	p. 24, Bonus Dialogue	
	p. 25, Words & Questions	p. 27, Phrases p. 28, Sentences
	p. 26, 27, Pronunciation Drill	p. 30, Vocabulary
	p. 29, Statements	p. 37, 38, 39, 40, 41
	p. 31, 32, 33, 34, 35, 36	
	p. 41, Idioms	

Week	Chapter in Class	Exercises (at Home)
	(THREE)	
5-7	p. 43, Episodes 1, 2	p. 44, Drawings & Dialogues
	p. 45, Episodes 3, 4	p. 45, Drawings & Dialogue
	p. 46, Episode 5	p. 46, Drawings & Dialogue
	p. 47, 48, 49	p. 49, 50
	p. 51, 52, 53, 54, 55	
	p. 56, 57, 58, 59, 60, 61, 62	p. 63, 64, 65, 66, 67
	p. 68, Idioms	
	(FOUR)	
	p. 71, Episodes 1, 2	p. 72, Drawings & Dialogue
	p. 72, Episodes 3, 4	p. 73, Drawings & Dialogue
	p. 74, 75	p. 76, A & B
	p. 77, 78, 79, 80	p. 77, Sentences
	p. 82, 83, 84, 85	p. 81, Vocabulary & Numbers
	p. 88, 89 - p. 94, Idioms & Traffic Signs	p. 86, 87
		p. 90, 91, 92, 93
	(FIVE)	
	p. 97-8, Episodes 1, 2	p. 98, Drawing & Dialogue
	p. 98, 99, Episodes 3, 4	
	p. 99, Episode 5	p. 100, Drawing & Dialogue
	p. 101, 102, 103	p. 103, A & B
	p. 104, 105, 106, 107	p. 104, Sentences
	p. 109, 110, 111, 112, 113, 114, 115, 116, 117	p. 108, Vocabulary
		p. 118, 119, 220, 221, 222, 223, 224, 225
	p. 126, 127, 128, 129	
	p. 130, 131, Idioms & Poems	

Week	Chapter in Class	Exercises (at Home)

(SIX)

8-10

p. 133-4, Episodes 1, 2 — p. 134, Drawing & Dialogue

p. 134-5, Episodes 3, 4 — p. 135, Drawing & Dialogue

p. 136-8, Pronunciation — p. 136, Words & Questions
p. 140, 141, 142, 143, 144 — p. 138-9, A & B - p. 139-40, Sentences
p. 145, 146, 147, 148, 149 — p. 144, Vocabulary A & B
p. 150, 151, 152, 153, 154, 155 — p. 155, 156, 157, 158, 159
p. 160, 161, Idioms

(SEVEN)

p. 163-4, Episodes 1, 2 — p. 164, Drawing & Dialogue

p. 164-5, Episodes 3, 4, 5 — p. 166, Drawing & Dialogue Words & Questions
p. 167, 168
p. 170, 171, 172, 173, 174, 175, 176, 177 — p. 168, A, 169, B, p. 169-70, Sentences
p. 177, Vocabulary
p. 178, 179, 180, 181, 182, 183, 184, 185, 186, 187 — p. 187, 189, 190, 191, 192, 193
p. 193, Idioms

(EIGHT)

11-12

p. 195-6, Episodes 1, 2 — p. 196, Drawing & Dialogue

196-7, Episodes 3, 4, 5 — p. 197, Drawing & Dialogue

p. 198, 199, 200 — p. 198, Words & Questions
p. 202, 203 — p. 200, A - p. 201-2, B & Sentences

Week	Chapter in Class	Exercises (at Home)
	(EIGHT cont.)	
11-12 (cont.)	p. 204, 205, 206, 207, 208, 209, 210, 211, 212, 123, 214, 215 p. 222, Idioms, p. 223 (NINE)	p. 203-4, Vocabulary p. 215, 216, 217, 218, 219, 220, 221, 222
	p. 225, 226, Episodes 1, 2 p. 226, 227, Episodes 3, 4 p. 228, 229, Episodes 5, 5 p. 230, 231, 232 p. 234, 235, 236, 237, 238, 239, 240, 241, 242, 243, 244, 245, 246 p. 254, Idioms	p. 226, Drawing & Dialogue p. 227, Drawing & Dialogue p. 228, Drawing & Dialogue p. 229, Words & Questions p. 232, A & B, p.232, Sentences p. 246, 247, 248, 249, 250, 251, 252, 253, 254
	(TEN)	
13-14	p. 257-8, Episodes 1, 2 p. 258-9, Episode 3 p. 259, 260, 261, 262 p. 263, 264, 265, 266 p. 268, 269, 270, 271, 272, 273, 274 p. 279, Idioms	p. 258, Drawing & Dialogue p. 259, Drawing & Dialogue p. 262, Words & Questions p. 266, A, p. 267-8, B, Sentences p. 274, 275, 276, 277, 278, 279
15	Review & Final Evaluation	

FIVE WEEKS SUMMER SYLLABUS FOR READING COMPREHENSION

TEXT: *Phase Two: Let's Read*

Week	Chapter in Class	Exercises (at Home)
	Introduction	
	(ONE)	
	p. 2, I-II- A.B.C. p. 6-7, Grammar	p. 4, D., E., & F.; p. 4-5, III p. 5, IV: A. & B.; p. 8, A; p. 9, B; p. 18-19, X; p. 20
1	(TWO)	
	p. 22-23	p. 24, E. & F.; p25, G. & H.; p.27-29, IV, A. & B.;
	p. 29-30, Grammar	p. 31-33, VI; 34-36, VII; p. 36-40, VII; p. 40-46 X; p. 47, B. & C.
	(THREE)	
	p. 50-51	p. 51 A. & B.; p. 52 C. & D.; p. 55-56, IV: A. & B.; p. 60, 63, 65, 67-68 IX;
2	p. 57, 58, 59, 60 Grammar	p. 69-70, 72, 73, C.; p.73 X, A.; p. 75

Week	Chapter in Class	Exercises (at Home)

	(FOUR)
	
	p. 77-78
	p.83-84, Grammar
		p. 79 D. & E., p. 80 F.,
		   G., H., & I.; p. 82 B.,
		   86 B., p. 89 VIII A.,
		p.92-94, IX: A.; p. 97,
		X.:A.; p. 99

	Mid-Term Progress Evaluation	
	(FIVE) p. 101-102 p. 108, 109, 110, Grammar	p. 103, A.B.C.D.; p. 105 III, p. 107 B; p. 113 VII; p. 115 VIII, p. 122 C.; p. 123 X. A.; 124 C.',
3		
	(SIX) P. 127-128 p. 134, 135, 136 Grammar	p. 129 A.B.C.D.; p. 132 IV A., p. 139 VII; p. 141 VIII; p. 145 IX, p. 149 C.; p. 151 X. B. C.
	(SEVEN) p. 153, 154, 155 p. 159, 160, 161, Grammar	p. 155 II, A.B.; p. 156 C.D.E., p. 159 B.; p. 161 VI; p. 165 VII, p. 168 C.; p. 172 B.; p. 174 C., p. 176 C.; p. 177 D.

Week	Chapter in Class	Exercises (at Home)
4	(EIGHT) p. 178-180 p. 185-186, Grammar	p. 180 II. A. through H., p. 182 III; p. 183 IV. A., p. 186 VI. A.; p. 188 VII; p. 194 A., 199 X. A.; p.200 D
5	(NINE) p. 201-202 p. 207, 208, 209, Grammar	p. 203 II; p. 205 III; p. 209 VI, p. 213 VIII, A.; p. 216 IX, A., p. 222 X, B.; p. 223 E., p. 226 II, A. B.; p. 227 III A., p. 229 IV, A.; p. 233 VII, p. 234 VIII; p. 241 X, A.; p. 242-243 D.E.
	Review & Final Evaluation	

Note: Explain each chapter's title page (*Words to Remember*), prior to starting on chapter proper. The above outline is not intended as a minimum; conversely, it need not be covered completely. As many of the chapter sections ought to be completed as the time permits. Exercises listed here may be assigned as homework; those not listed may be done in class, if time permits.

FALL OR SPRING SEMESTER
SYLLABUS FOR READING COMPREHENSION

TEXT: *Phase Two; Let's Read*

Week	Chapter in Class	Exercises (at Home)
	Introduction	
	(ONE)	
1-4	p. 2, I-II, A.B.C. 6-7, Grammar	p. 4, D. E. F., III; p. 5-6, IV: A. & B.; p. 8, A.; p.9, B.; p. 19, X: B.;p. 20
	(TWO)	
	p. 23,24 29,30, Grammar	p. 24-25, E. F. G. H.; p. 27-28, IV, A. & B. 31, 32, 33, 34, 35, 36, 37, 38, 39, 40, 46 X. A. B.; p. 47 C.
	(THREE)	
5-7	p. 50-51 57,60, Grammar	p. 51 A. B.; p. 52 C.D.; p. 55-56, IV A. & B.; p. 60-68 VI-IX; p. 69, 70, 72, C.; p. 73 X: A.; p. 75

Week	Chapter in Class	Exercises (at Home)
	(FOUR)	
	p. 77,78 83,84, Grammar	p. 79 D. E.; p. 80 F. G.H. I.; p. 82 B., 86 B., 89 VIII A.; p. 92 IX: A.; p. 97 X: A.; p. 99
	(FIVE)	
	p. 101, 102 108, 109, 110, Grammar	p. 103, A. B. C. D.; p. 105 III; p. 107 B.; p. 113 VII; p 115 VIII; p. 122 C.; p. 123 X, A.; p. 124 C
8-10	(SIX)	
	p. 127,128 134, 135, 136, Grammar	p. 129 A.B.C.D.; p. 132 IV, A.; 139 VII; p. 141 VIII; p. 145 IX; 149 C; p. 151 X, B.C.
	(SEVEN)	
	p. 153, 154, 154, 155 159, 160, 161	p. 155 II, A.B.; p. 156 C.D.E.; 159 B.; p. 161 VI; p. 166 VIII; 168 C.; p. 172 B.; p. 175 C.; 176 C.; p. 177 D.
11-12	(EIGHT)	
	p. 178, 180 185, 186, Grammar	p. 180 II, A.B.C.D.E.F.G.H., 182 III; p. 183 IV, A.; 186 VI, A.; p. 188 VII; p. 194 A.; 199 X, A.; p. 200 D.

Week	Chapter in Class	Exercises (at Home)
	(NINE)	
	p. 201, 202 207, 208, 209, Grammar	p. 203 II; p. 204 II; p. 209 VI; 213 VIII, A.; p. 216 IX, A.; 222 X, B.; p. 223 E.
13-14	(TEN)	
	p. 224, 225 230, 231, Grammar	p. 226 II, A.B.; p. 227 III, A.; 229 IV, A.; p. 233 VII; 234 VIII; p. 241 X, A.; p. 242, 243 D.E.
15	Review & Final Evaluation	

Note: Explain each chapter's title page (*Words to Remember*), prior to starting on chapter proper. The above outline is not intended as a minimum; it need not be covered completely. As many of the chapter sections ought to be completed as time permits. Exercises listed here may be assigned as homework; those not listed may be done in class.

FIVE WEEKS SUMMER SYLLABUS
FOR WRITING

TEXT: *Phase Three; Let's Write*

Week	Chapter in Class	Exercises (at Home)	Composition (at Home)
	(ONE)		
1	p. 2, A. Composition 6-9, Spelling Rules 22, 23, 24, 25, 26	p. 3-4 C. & D., p. 4 E. 10 D. & E., p. 11, 26, 27	
	(TWO)		
	p. 32-34, A. Composition 40, 41, 42, 43, 44, 45, 46	p. 34, 35, 38 B., 40 B., 46, 47, 48, 49, 52 B., 53 B.	p. 56 C. 55 IX, X
2	(THREE)		
	p. 58 A. Composition 66, 67, 68, 69	p. 59 B., 62, 63, 65 B., 70 D., 70, 71, 72; p. 74, VI, A. & B.; p. 76 VII A.	p. 79 IX, X 80 C.

Week	Chapter in Class	Exercises (at Home)	Composition (at Home)
	(FOUR)		
2 (cont.)	p. 82 A. 90, 91, 92, 93, 94	p. 83, 85, II, A., 86, 87 94, 95, 96, 97, 98, 99, 102, 103	p. 106 IX, X 107 A., B., C.
	(FIVE)		
3	p. 109 A. Composition 117 IV, to 122	p. 109 B., 110, 111, 112, 113 C., 115 III: A., 115 B., 122, 123, 126 VI A., 127 B., 130 VIII A.	p. 130 IX, A., 131 A., b., C.

MID-TERM PROGRESS EVALUATION

	(SIX)		
	p. 136 A. Composition 144, 145, 146	p. 138, 139, 140, 141, 142, 144 B., 149 B, 149 B, 150, 151	p. 153 IX A., 155 D.
	(SEVEN)		
4	p. 157 A. Composition 165, 166, 167	p. 161, 162, 165 B., 167, 168, 169, 171 B., 172 C., 173 VII A., 174 B.	177 IX A., & B.X, A., p. 178 B.

Week	Chapter in Class	Exercises (at Home)	Composition (at Home)
	(EIGHT)		
4 (cont.)	p. 183 A. Composition 189, 190	p. 185 B., 188 B., 191 D., 195 C., 196 VII A.	p. 201 IX A., B., X, A., 202 B.
	(NINE)		
5	p. 204 A. & B. Composition 205, 206, 207, 213, 214, 215, 216, 217, 218, 219, 220, 221	p. 208, 209, E., 210 B., 212 B., 221 E., 222 VI A., 223 B., 225 VII A., 227 B.	p.226 VIII A., 228 IX A., 229 X A., B., 230 D.
	(TEN)		
	p. 232 A. Composition 238, 239, 240, 241, 242	p. 235 B., 237 B., 243 C., 245 V, 247 B., 249 VII A., 250 B., 252 B.	p. 254 IX, X A., B., 225 C.

REVIEW & FINAL EVALUATION

Note: Explain each chapter's title page (*Words to Remember*), prior to starting on chapter proper. The above outline is not intended as a minimum; conversely, it need not be covered completely. As many of the chapter sections ought to be completed as the time permits. Exercises listed here may be assigned as homework; those not listed may be done in class, if time permits.

FALL OR SPRING SEMESTER
SYLLABUS FOR WRITING

TEXT: *Phase Three: Let's Write*

Week	Chapter in Class	Exercises (at Home)	Composition (at Home)
	(ONE)		
1-4	p. 2, A. Composition 6-9, Spelling Rules 22, 23, 24, 25, 26	p. 3-4 C. & D., p. 5 E. 10 D. & E., p. 11, 26, 27	
	(TWO)		
	p. 32-34, A. Composition 40, 41, 42, 43, 44, 45, 46	p. 34, 35, 38 B., 40 B., 46, 47, 48, 49, 52 B., 53 B.	p. 56 C. 55 IX, X
	(THREE)		
5-7	p. 58 A. Composition 66, 67, 68, 69	p. 59 B., 62, 63, 65 B., 70 D., 70, 71, 72, 73; p. 74, VI:	p. 79 IX, X 80 C.

Week	Chapter in Class	Exercises (at Home)	Composition (at Home)
	(FOUR)	A. & B.; p. 76, VII: A.	
	p. 82 A. 90, 91, 92, 93, 94	p. 83, 84, 85, II, A., 86, 87 94, 95, 96, 97, 98, 99, 102,	p. 106 IX, X 107 A., B., C.
	(FIVE)	103	
8-10	p. 109 A. Composition 117 IV, to 122	p. 109 B., 110, 111, 112, 114 C., 115 III A., 116 B., 122, 123, 126 VI A., 127 B., 129 VIII A.	p. 130 IX, A., 131 A., B., C.

MID-TERM PROGRESS EVALUATION

Week	Chapter in Class	Exercises (at Home)	Composition (at Home)
	(SIX)	p. 138, 139, 140, 141, 142, 144 B., 148 A, 149 B, 150, 151	p. 153 IX A., 155 D.
	p. 136 A. Composition 144, 145, 146		
	(SEVEN)		
11-12	p. 157 A. Composition 165, 166, 167	p. 161, 162, 164 B., 167, 168, 169, 171 B., 172 C., 173 VII A., 174 B.	p. 177 IX A., & B.X, A., p. 178 B.

Week	Chapter in Class	Exercises (at Home)	Composition (at Home)
	(EIGHT)		
	p. 182 A. Composition 189, 190	p. 186 B., 189 B., 192 D., 196 C., 197 VII A.	p. 200 IX A., B., X, A., 202 B.
	(NINE)		
13-14	p. 204 A. & B. Composition 205, 206, 207, 213, 214, 215, 216, 217, 218, 219, 220, 221	p. 208, 209, E., 210 B., 212 B., 221 E., 222 VI A., 223 B., 225 VII A., 227 B.	p. 226 VIII A., 228 IX A., 229 X A., B., 230 D.
	(TEN)		
	p. 232 A. Composition 238, 239, 240, 241, 242	p. 236 B., 238 B., 244 C., 246 V, 248 B., 250 VII A., 251 B., 252 B.	p. 254 IX, X A., B., 225 C.
15	REVIEW & FINAL EVALUATION		

Note: Explain each chapter's title page (*Words to Remember*), prior to starting on chapter proper. The above outline is not intended as a minimum; conversely, it need not be covered completely.   As many of the chapter sections ought to be completed as the time permits. Exercises listed here may be assigned as homework; those not listed may be done in class, if time permits.

FIVE WEEKS OF INTERMEDIATE CONVERSATION & COMPOSITION SYLLABUS

TEXT: *Phase Four; Let's Continue*

Week	Chapter in Class	Exercises (at Home)	Composition (at Home)
	(ONE)		
1	p. 1, 2, 3, Dialogue 4, 5, Narrative 14, 15, 16, 17, 18, 22, 23, 24, 25, 26	p. 5, 6, 7, 8, 9, 10, 19, 20, 26, 27, 28	p. 11, 12, 13, 20, 21, 22, 28, 29, 30
	(TWO)		
2	p. 31, 32, 33, 34, 35, 43, 44, 45, 46, 47, 51, 52, 53, 54	p. 35, 36, 37, 38, 39, 40, 48, 49, 50, 51	p. 40, 41, 42, 47, 48 p. 54, 55, 56, 58, 59, 60, 61
	(THREE)		
3	p. 63, 64, 65, 66, 67, 74, 75, 76, 77, 78, 81, 82, 83, 84, 85	p. 68, 69, 70, 71, 72	p. 72, 73 p. 79, 80 p. 86, 87, 88

Week	Chapter in Class	Exercises (at Home)	Composition (at Home)
	(FOUR)		
4	p. 89, 90, 91, 92, 100, 101, 102, 103, 104, 105	p. 78, 79, 83, 84	p. 98, 99, 100, 106, 107, 108, 109,
		p. 93, 94, 95, 96, 97, 98	111, 112, 115, 116, 117
	p. 108, 109, 110, 113, 114	p. 105, 106	
		p. 110, 111	
	(FIVE)		
5	p. 119, 120, 121, 122, 123, 130, 131, 132, 133, 134, 135, 136, 137, 140, 141, 142, 143	p. 123, 124, 125 126, 127	p. 127, 128, 129, 130, 139, 140 p. 144, 145, 146,
		p. 137, 138, 139	147, 148, 149
		p. 143, 144, 145, 146	

REVIEW & FINAL EVALUATION

Note: Explain each chapter's title page (*Words to Remember),* prior to starting on chapter proper. The above outline is not intended as a minimum; conversely, it need not be covered completely. As many of the chapter sections ought to be completed as the time permits. Exercises listed here may be assigned as homework; those not listed may be done in class, if time permits.

FALL OR SPRING SEMESTER
INTERMEDIATE CONVERSATION
& COMPOSITION SYLLABUS

TEXT: *Phase Four; Let's Continue*

Week	Chapter (in Class)	Exercises (at Home)	Composition (at Home)
	(ONE)		
1-3	p. 1, 2, 3, Dialogue 4, 5, Narrative 14, 15, 16, 17, 18, 22, 23, 24, 25, 26	p. 5, 6, 7, 8, 9, 10, 19, 20, 26, 27, 28	p. 11, 12, 13, 20, 21, 22, 28, 29, 30
	(TWO)		
4-6	p. 31, 32, 33, 34, 35, 43, 44, 45, 46, 47, 51, 52, 53, 54	p. 35, 36, 37, 38, 39, 40, 48, 49, 50, 51	p. 40, 41, 42, 47, 48 p. 54, 55, 56, 58, 59, 60, 61
	(THREE)		
7-9	p. 63, 64, 65, 66, 67, 74, 75, 76, 77, 78, 81, 82, 83, 84, 85	p. 68, 69, 70, 71, 72 p. 78, 79, 83, 84	p. 72, 73 p. 79,80 P. 86, 87, 88

Week	Chapter (in Class)	Exercises (at Home)	Composition (at Home)
	(FOUR)		
10-12	p. 89, 90, 91, 92, 100, 101, p. p.102, 103, 104, 105,	p. 93, 94, 95, 96, 97, 98 p. 105, 106	p. 98, 99, 100, 106, 107, 108, 109, 111, 112, 115, 116, 117
	p. 108, 109, 110, 113, 114	p. 110, 111	
	(FIVE)		
13-14	p. 119, 120, 121, 122, 123, 130, 131, 132, 133, 134, 135, 136, 137, 140, 141, 142, 143	p.123,124, 125, 126, 127 p. 137, 138, 139 p. 143, 144, 145, 146	p. 127, 128, 129, 130, 139, 140 p. 144, 145, 146, 147, 148, 149
15	REVIEW & FINAL EVALUATION		

NOTE: Explain each chapter's title page (*Words to Remember*), prior to starting on chapter proper. The above outline is not intended as a minimum; conversely, it need not be covered completely. As many of the chapter sections ought to be completed as the time permits. Exercise listed here may be assigned as homework; those not listed may be done in class, if time permits

FIVE WEEKS OF ADVANCED
CONVERSATION & COMPOSITION
SYLLABUS

Week	Chapter in Class	Exercises (at Home)	Composition (at Home)
	(SIX)		
1	p. 151, 152, 153, 154, 155, 161,162, 163,	p. 156, 157, 159	p. 168, 169
			p. 174, 175, 176
	164, 165, 166, 167	p. 160, 161, 167, 168, 169, 170, 171	p. 179, 180, 181
	p. 171, 172, 193, 174 177, 178	p. 178, 179	
	(SEVEN)		
2	p. 183, 184, 185 186, 187	p. 187, 188, 189, 190, 191	p. 200, 201
	p. 192, 193, 194, 195, 196, 197, 201, 202, 203, 205, 206	p. 198, 199, 203, 204	

Week	Chapter in Class	Exercises (at Home)	Composition (at Home)
3	(EIGHT)		p. 206, 207, 208
		p. 212, 213, 314	
	p. 209, 210, 211, 212, 217, 218, 219, 220, 221, 222, 223	224, 225, 226, 227, 229, 230, 231	p. 215, 216
			p. 233, 234, 236, 237, 238
	p. 227, 228, 229, 232, 233, 235, 236		
4	(NINE)		p. 253, 254
		p. 243, 244, 246, 247, 248, 252, 253, 256, 257	p. 259, 260, 261
	p. 239, 240, 241, 242, 244, 245, 246, 248, 249, 250, 251, 252, 254, 255, 256, 258, 259		
5	(TEN)		p. 269, 270, 271, 272
		p. 266, 267, 268, 269	
	p. 263, 264, 265, 273, 274, 275, 276		p. 279, 280, 281
		p. 277, 278, 279	
			p. 285, 286
		282, 283, 284	

COMPREHENSIVE REVIEW &   FINAL EVALUATION

Note: Explain each chapter's title page (*Words to Remember),* prior to starting on chapter proper. The above outline is not intended as a minimum; conversely, it need not be covered completely. As many of the chapter sections ought to be completed as the time permits. Exercises listed here may be assigned as homework; those not listed may be done I class, if time permits.

FALL OR SPRING SEMESTER
ADVANCED CONVERSATION & COMPOSITION
SYLLABUS

TEXT: *Phase Four; Let's Continue*

Week	Chapter in Class	Exercises (at Home)	Composition (at Home)
	(SIX)		
1-3	p. 151, 152, 153, 154, 155, 161,162, 163,	p. 156, 157, 159	p. 168, 169
			p. 174, 175, 176
	164, 165, 166, 167	p. 160, 161, 167, 168, 169, 170, 171	p. 179, 180, 181
	p. 171, 172, 193, 174 177, 178	p. 178, 179	
	(SEVEN)		
4-6	p. 183, 184, 185 186, 187	p. 187, 188, 189, 190, 191	p. 200, 201
	p. 192, 193, 194, 195, 196, 197, 201, 202, 203, 205, 206	p. 198, 199, 203, 204	

Week	Chapter in Class	Exercises (at Home)	Composition (at Home)
7-9	(EIGHT)		
	p. 209, 210, 211, 212, 217, 218, 219, 220, 221, 222, 223	p. 212, 213, 314 224, 225, 226, 227, 229, 230, 231	p. 206, 207, 208 215, 216
	p. 227, 228, 229, 232, 233, 235, 236		p. 233, 234, 236, 237, 238
10-12	(NINE)		
	p. 239, 240, 241, 242, 244, 245, 246, 248, 249, 250, 251, 252, 254, 255, 256, 258, 259	p. 243, 244, 246, 247, 248, 252, 253, 256, 257	p. 253, 254 p. 259, 260, 261
13-14	(TEN)		
	p. 263, 264, 265, 273, 274, 275, 276	p. 266, 267, 268, 269 p. 277, 278, 279 p. 282, 283, 284	p. 269, 270, 271, 272 p. 279, 280, 281 p. 285, 286

15   COMPREHENSIVE REVIEW & FINAL EVALUATION

Note: Explain each chapter's title page (*Words to Remember*), prior to starting on chapter proper. The above outline is not intended as a minimum; conversely, it need not be covered completely. As many of the chapter sections ought to be completed as the time permits. Exercises listed here may be assigned as homework; those not listed may be done I class, if time permits.

STRUCTURED PROGRESS AND SCOPE OF THE ESL "LET'S SERIES"

Phase Zero Plus: Let's Begin

Week	Basic Skill Feature	Skill Practice	Expected Functional Skill Acquisition
1	Penmanship	practice and learn the alphabet spelling and writing practice syllabification and important sounds	Cursive Writing
2	Questions	*What/is — how/ where*	Greetings
	Present Time	verbs *have* and *be*	Basic Converation
	Contractions	*we've/you've/ they've/what's it's,* etc.	Asking Questions Self-introduction Meeting People Introducing People

Week	Basic Skill Feature	Skill Practice	Expected Functional Skill Acquistion
3	Affirmative statement	Noun Phrase + Verb Phrase	Daily Activities
	Demonstratives:	*this/that*	Social Courtesies
	Singular and Plural		Occupational Activities
	Negatives	no/not	School
4	Personal Pronoun Subject	*I/you/he/she/it/ we/you/they*	Meeting People
	Demonstrative Pronouns	*this/that/here/ there*	Discussing Occupations
	Questions with	*what*	Telling Nation- alities
	Negative Contractions:	*isn't/aren't*	
	Nationalities		
5	Possessive Adjectives:	my/your/his/her/ our/your/their	Telling Time
	Present Con- tinuous of Verbs	*be + Verb + ing*	Counting
	Numbers	From 0 (zero) to 20 (twenty)	Making Affir- mative Negative Statements
	Telling time	*when?/early/ late/on time/ o'clock/always/ never today*	Habitual Activities

Week	Basic Skill Feature	Skill Practice	Expected Functional Skill Acquistion
6	Possessive Pronouns	mine/yours/his/ hers/ours/yours/ theirs	Preparing Food
	Question:	whose?	Identifying Household Utensils
	Days Of The Week	*Monday* Through *Sunday*	More Numbers
	One and Many	Singular and Plural	Identifying People
	Ordinal Numbers:	*first, second,* etc.	Naming Days Of The Week
7	Command, Polite Request:	would you..?/ shall we..?/ let's..?	Talking About Animals
	Demonstratives:	these/those	Making Requests and Giving Commands
	Adjectives:	Words that Describe	Reminders and Responses
	Use Of	*where*/tag questions	More Numbers
	The Seasons	January through December	
	Object Pronouns		
8	Use of	*and/but/or*	Telling Dates and Seasons
	The Weather:	*cold/warm/mild/ it rains/it snows/it's windy/it's hot*	Making Daily Plans

Week	Basic Skill Feature	Skill Practice	Expected Functional Skill Acquistion
8 (con't)	Directions:	North/South/ East/West	Talking About Weather
			Calendar Study
9	Adjectives		Shapes and Sizes of People and Objects
	Compound Sentences		Physical Description
	The Human Body		
10	Colors:	*brown/red/white/ black/yellow,*etc.	Shopping for Groceries
	Use of:	*and/too-- everybody/ nobody*	Money Expressions Price and Rates
		as...as	Identifying Food Products
		around/in/on/to/ with	Identifying Colors
			Clothing Items
11	Object Pronouns		Family and Relatives
	Direct and Indirect Object		Identifying Occupations
	Comparatives of Adjectives and Adverbs		Pricing Items

Week	Basic Skill Feature	Skill Practice	Expected Functional Skill Acquistion
11	Use of:	more/bigger/ better/than *too* +Adverb	Food character-istics
12	Review of	*wh* - questions	The Home and Its Components
	Positions	above/below/ under/on top of/ in front of/next to/beside/ behind/	
	Use of:	a/an/the/some	
			Giving Direc-tions
	Comparison of Adjectives and Adverbs		Household Chores and Activities
13	Directions:	right/left/ straight/ahead/ around the corner/opposite/ follow/block/ across	Getting Around Asking for Directions
	Review	the use of *in/on/ at* with *time/*and *place*	Giving Direc-tions
			Identifying Places

Week	Basic Skill Feature	Skill Practice	Expected Functional Skill Acquistion
14	Adjectives and Adverbs Comparison Use of:	*alike/different/ the same/ similar/turn on/ turn off*	Expressing Amounts and Quantities Talking About Activities Writing Short Dialogue Writing (Describing) Short Situation
15	Comprehensive Review and Evaluations		Survival Knowledge of English

STRUCTURED PROGRESS AND SCOPE

Phase One: Let's Converse

Week	Basic Skill Feature	Skill Practice	Expected Functional Skill Acquistion
1	Basic Sounds Greetings	Intonation - Sound Patterns	Correct Pronunciation of Unusual Sounds
	Occupations and Nationalities	Dialogue About School & Occupations Listen and Talk	Introduction of Self and Others
	Recreation Present Tense	Dialogue and Vocabulary	Discuss Recreational Activities and Nationalities
		Verbs *be* and *have*	Basic Conversation
2	Questions and Negatives	"yes" and "no" response	Asking Questions
	Affirmative Statement	Listen and Talk	Responding Positively and Negativly
	Idioms	Noun Phrase + Verb Phrase	
	Weather and Recreation		
	Questions	Weather Related to Activities	

Week	Basic Skill Feature	Skill Practice	Expected Functional Skill Acquistion
2 (con't)	Present Time	*what?*	Weather Related Recreational Activities
	Nouns	Present Continuous	Planning Recreational Activities
		Count Nouns and Non-count Nouns	
	Numbers	Zero (0) to Ten (10)	
3	Days of the Week	Repetition of Question - Response	Talking About Activities
	Months and Seasons	Listen/Talk Vocabulary Sentences	Social Language
	Present and Present Continuous	Exercises	Reminders and Responses
	Spelling (Singular - Plural)		
4	Adverbials of Frequency	Listen and Talk	Telling Time and Making Appointments
	Adverbials of Time	*how often?* *When?* *What?*	Describing Events and Weather
	Questions in Reference to *things, occupations,* or *animals*	Pronunciation of Idioms	Talking About Occupations

Week	Basic Skill Feature	Skill Practice	Expected Functional Skill Acquistion
5	Numbers - (11 to 100) eleven to one hundred	Third Person Sing. add "s" - some - "ies" - use with *does* in Questions	Shopping for School Supplies - Fruit, etc.
	Review of Present Time		Habitual Actions
	Indefinite Pronouns	Listen and Talk	Common Courtesies
	Question Words	every/any/some/ no/what/where/ who/when/why/ how/how come	Finding Out and Talking About People
	Adjectives words that describe colors	Pronunciation and Idioms	Selecting Colors
6	Numbers (101 to 1000) one hundred one to one thousand	Practice Adding and Subtracting	Asking for Direction
		Give Distances and Measure -	Getting Car Assistance
	Expressions of Measure: Time and Metric Linear	Compare Metric to Yard Measure	Talk about Past Experiences
		Listen and Talk	Talk about Travel
	Simple Past Tense	Drill Present and Past Tense in complete sentences using most *verbs* learned from *plurals* of nouns	Describe Your Possessions
	Irregular Verbs		Identify Traffic Signs
	Continuous Past		

Week	Basic Skill Feature	Skill Practice	Expected Functional Skill Acquistion
6 (con't)	Count and Noncount Nouns Prepositions with Time and Place Possesive Determiners	on/in/at/to Questions with *when?* and *where?* Answer Question *whose?* Nouns with *"s"* Idioms	
7	The Clock Review Past Tense Future Time Request - Question About Future Adverbials of Place/Manner/Time	Pronunciation of Time *Elements* Compare and Practice Past and Present Tense will/ I'll - going to *will?* or *won't?* Listen/Talk where?/how?/when? idioms	Medical Care and Receiving Assistance Telling Time Plan for Future Activities Tell Parts of Human Body
8	Job Related Words The Present Perfect: Conversational Past Verb *get*	Words and Questions Listen/Talk Study Comparative Exercise: *present/past/ Present perfect*	Getting a Job Interviewing Handling a Telephone Call Expressions of Time

Week	Basic Skill Feature	Skill Practice	Expected Functional Skill Acquistion
8 (con't)	Adverbials of Frequency	Practice various uses of *get* how often?	
9	Pronouns as: Object, Personal Possessive Adjective Possessive Pronoun	Listen/Talk Statements and Sentences Study *word usage* Idioms	Telling Time, Date, Quantity Solving Problems and Reasoning Telling about Things Past & Present
	Very, Too, So + Adjective		Going Out Socially
10	Modal/Auxiliaries	Listen/Talk *words* and *questions*	Tell about Food and Going Out To Eat
	Past Perfect Tense	Study Comparison of Tenses - *present/future/past*	Ordering Food in a Restaurant
	Comparison	as...as Idioms	Commands and Polite Requests

Week	Basic Skill Feature	Skill Practice	Expected Functional Skill Acquistion
11	Past Perfect Continuous	Words and Questions about Banking	Banking and Money Talk
	Adjectives and Comparatives/ Superlatives	Listen/Talk Exercises	Making Deposits and Withdrawals
	Adverbials of Manner	*-er/est*	Savings and Checking Accounts
		at/by/in/for/ during/since/ before/after/until	
	Prepositions of Time	*(till)*	Asking people to do things
	Compound Nouns		
12	Prepositional Phrases	at/by/on/in/with	Going Shopping
			Experiencing Department Store
	Two-Word Verbs	*Constructing sentences*	
			Money Talk
	Clauses Modifying Verbs	although/as soon as/because/ before, *etc.*	
		yet/lately/ already/finally/	Buying Gifts
	Modifiers of Verbs	*still*	

Week	Basic Skill Feature	Skill Practice	Expected Functional Skill Acquistion
13	Infinitive Phrases	Practicing sentences with verbs *be/ continue/forget/ learn/*etc.	Brief Outlines of: U.S. History
	Infinitive as Object Complement	Verb + *ing*	U.S. Geography U.S. Government
	Gerund as Noun		
14	Participle as Modifier	educat*ed*/tri*ed*/ decid*ed*, etc.	Discuss: Declaration of Independence/ Bill of Rights/ The Congress, etc.
	Verbs that take Participles as Modifiers	Practice sentences *have/must/could/* etc.	Ability to Interview and Apply for Citizenship
		Idioms Study Application for Citizenship	

Week	Basic Skill Feature	Skill Practice	Expected Functional Skill Acquistion
15	Comprehensive Review and Oral Evaluation		Socially Conversant
			Hold Your Own in Comprehension and Conversation on Matters Pertaining to Personal Interest More than Survival Knowledge of English

STRUCTURED PROGRESS AND SCOPE

Phase Two: Let's Read

Week	Basic Skill Feature	Skill Practice	Expected Functional Skill Acquistion
1	Parts of Speech	read & study sentences comprising	Recognition of Parts of Speech - Origin of English Words
	The Sentence	various parts of speech	
	The Paragraph	read exemplary paragraphs and	
	Roots and Prefixes	point out roots and prefixes	
		make goals explicit	
2	Present Time:	Read narrative Teacher reads,	Comprehension of Simple Narrative in the Present Time
	Habitual Action	Students listen-	
	General Action	Several times	
	Present Condition		
		Explain-then Students read	High Frequency Words and Cognates
	Personal Pronoun:	*I/you/he/she/it/ we/you/they*	Familiar Topics
		practice vocabulary	Describe Routine Behavior

Week	Basic Skill Feature	Skill Practice	Expected Functional Skill Acquistion
2 (con't)	Declarative Sentence and Determiners:	*a/an/the*	
	Possessives	*my/your/our/his/ their*	
	Demonstratives	*this/that/these/ those*	
3	Present Continuous Adverbials: of Time	*in the morning/ every weekend/ minutes later/* etc.	Selections of Simple Magazine & Newspaper Articals
	of Frequency	*usually/always/ never/*etc.	
4	Words that Describe	*yellow/green/ orange/*etc.	Read Jokes, Announcements of Coming Events - Adds - Letters to the Editor, etc.
	Adjectives	*good/modest/ small/*etc.	
		explain pictographs	Read Simple Poetry
		read against time	for Surface Meaning and Structure

Week	Basic Skill Feature	Skill Practice	Expected Functional Skill Acquistion
5	Simple Past and Past Continuous	every-/-body	Read Structures Encountered in Non-Technical Text -
	Indefinite Pronouns:	any-/-one	
		some-/-thing	
		no-/what?/ where?/who?/ where?/	Free Reading -
	Question Words:	why?/how?	
6	Comparative and Superlative	*older - oldest Prettier - Prettiest,* etc.	Reading Simple Material *against* Time -
			Compete Against Self
		read timed diagnostic vocabulary exercises-some outside reading	Read Simple Poetry For Deep Meaning
7	Words Express- ing Obligation:	should/ought/ had/better/had to	Tell Meaning of Selected Outside Reading Material
	Prepositions:	in/on/at/to	
		read and discuss poem	
	Possessive Determiners:	*my/your/his/her/* etc.	

Week	Basic Skill Feature	Skill Practice	Expected Functional Skill Acquistion
8	Present Perfect	have + past Participle	Reading in Newspaper Articles Concerning Local News and Demestic Items - Discuss Intelligently
	Future Time	*will/'ll/shall/+ infinitive*	
	Request/ Question	read and discuss poetry	
	Possessive Pronoun:	*mine/yours/his/ hers/etc.*	
	Place/Manner and Time	*where?/when?/ how?*	
9	Past Perfect	*had + past participle* Outside Reading *good* > better	Read for Deep Meaning Poetry and Narrative Read in History
	Comparison Equal and Unequal Things	*bad* > worse	Diversification Skills Previewing Scanning
	Adjective (adverb)	*very/too/so/*etc. *and + too -and + so - but*	Selecting Skimming
10	Passive Voice	Study Words Synonyms and Antonyms	Read About Social Activities - Hobbies and Recreation
	Active Voice		
	Imperative Mood	Let's + Infinitive	More Reading in History
		Study Commands and Requests	

Week	Basic Skill Feature	Skill Practice	Expected Functional Skill Acquistion
11	Past Perfect Continuous Sequence of Tenses Condition	*had + been +* Verb + *ing* Words in Context the following, etc. if - would *the* in a *time* or *space* sequence	Read about Citizenship - Customs - Discuss Read for Pleasure - Stories - Poems
12	Relative Clause Relative Pronoun: as Subject as Object as Modifier of Noun	*who/whom/ which/*etc. read against time outside readings read and analyze narra-tive and poem	Read Instruc-tional Reading Material Read Collec-tions of Letters - Newspapers
13	Demonstratives: Relative Pronouns:	*this/that/these/ those* *whom/which/ that*	Expected to read all types of news articles with high frequency words

Week	Basic Skill Feature	Skill Practice	Expected Functional Skill Acquistion
13 (con't)		intensive classroom reading - assign corresponding outside reading	
14	Adverbs and Adverbial Phrases	where/when extensive outside reading	Timed: Vocabulary Reading Narrative Poetry For Meaning
15	Comprehensive Review and Evaluation		Reading with natural ease in a normal speed with the intention to derive deep meaning, 100 to 400 words per minute, 9th and 10th grade level - with *Translation* Beyond 200 w/ p/m Reading for special purpose preparing for the G.E.D. Exam or TOEFL

STRUCTURED PROGRESS AND SCOPE

Phase Three: Let's Write

Week	Basic Skill Feature	Skill Practice	Expected Functional Skill Acquistion
1	Study of the *Word*	recognition - discrimination - spelling-area of meaning root - stem - base prefix and suffix	Learn to recognize words and their derivatives for meaning
2	Mechanics of word structure and restructure	word in context structure - composition word formation change of meaning-change of parts of speech	Recognizing change in context Constructing words their synonyms and antonynms Familiarization with foreign word derivatives and low frequency vocabulary

Week	Basic Skill Feature	Skill Practice	Expected Functional Skill Acquistion
3	Simple Sentence	Making declarative statements asking Questions affirmative vs. negative imperative exclamatory	Writing simple sentences while choosing the more common words
4	Study of Sentence Structure: Punctuation	practice constructing simple sentence: Subject - Predicate period - capitalization question mark - exclamation mark	Paraphrasing outside reading material in simple terms
5	Compound Sentence Independent Clause Coordinators	practice constructing simple sentences and combining them into compound sentences while using *and/but/ for/nor/or/so/yet*	Writing short sentences the most familiar events and objects - for example: "A Day in Your Life" "The Person "You Love" "My Family"

Week	Basic Skill Feature	Skill Practice	Expected Functional Skill Acquistion
6	Parallelism Faulty Parallelism Punctuation Complex Sentence Main Clause Subordinate Clause	Study examples of correct writing semicolon - comma - hyphen compose complex sentences choosing common vocabulary	Writing About Daily Occurences in the present "On The Campus" "Why I Study" "I Want to be..." etc.
7	Relationships Subordination and Subordinators Punctuation	practice using subordinators of *time/place/ contrast/ purpose/cause/ manner and comparison* comma - colon - question marks	Selecting newspaper or magazine article for rewriting - using grammatical structures learned thus far

Week	Basic Skill Feature	Skill Practice	Expected Functional Skill Acquistion
8	Sequence of Tenses	adverbs of time: *after/always/at least/before/ during/earlier/* etc. practice constructions of sentences in sequential order	Writing about past events of personal intrests while using the tense constructions learned
9	The Tense: Present (continuous) Past (continuous) Present Perfect Past Perfect Future	practice constructions with sequential time limitations	Write about occupational plans and work using tense structures freely
10	Outline	listing related items in isolation	making an outline for purposes of preparing a composition
	Organization and Analysis	separating unrelated items	

Week	Basic Skill Feature	Skill Practice	Expected Functional Skill Acquistion
11	Topic Outline	writing short paragraphs and/or single words	Writing of a main topic idea with a composition in mind
	Topic Sentence Main Idea	preparing various topic sentences and describing the underlying idea	
	Elements of a Paragraph	topic sentence body and conclusion	Making an outline of a paragraph with all its elements
12	Coherence	practicing the coherance in paragraph composition	Writing a complete paragraph on a familiar topic
	Topic Sentence: Body:	main idea development of idea	Writing a critical paragraph based on selected reading material
	Concluding Sentence:	end of paragraph	
13	Transitional Phrases:	practice connecting sentences while using such expresions as *therefore/in conclusion/ furthermore/*etc.	Writing complete paragraphs on familiar topics while using sequential tenses and transitional phrases

Week	Basic Skill Feature	Skill Practice	Expected Functional Skill Acquistion
14	Composition	practicing the interrelationship of paragraphs to form a compo-sition	Writing short composition while using all transitional elements
	Types of Composition	practice essay writing, letters: formal informal etc. Term Paper	Composing short essays - writing various types of letters - writing a term paper
		Practice collect-ing data for writing term paper	
	Style - Form and Structure	practice the different styles of compositions *prose/dialogue/ letters/poetry*	Composing freely in varied styles and forms on familiar topics
15	Comprehensive Review and Evaluation		Writing Freely in any form or structure, with grammatical awareness and a familiarity of cultural terms such as: "red tape," "buy American," etc. - Discussing rea-sons for career choice, etc. Preparing for the G.E.D. Exam or TOEFL

STRUCTURED PROGRESS AND SCOPE

Phase Four: Let's Continue

Week	Basic Skill Feature	Skill Practice	Expected Functional Skill Acquistion
1	Two - Word Verbs	Practice constructing compositions, using two-word verbs Learn health related words	Discussing and writing on level of higher sophistication using low frequency words
2		Practice free composition Completing dialogues	
3	Two - Word Verbs	Learning about dental care Discussing the environment	Writing and discussing about health related topics discussing and writing about the environment

Week	Basic Skill Feature	Skill Practice	Expected Functional Skill Acquistion
3 (con't)		practice the use of special expressions related to physical and mental condition	Discuss the cowboy tradition while using two - word verbs
		sing songs	
4	Compound Prepositions	drug store related activities and words	Discussing and writing about the advantages of communication - Using compound prepositons
		learning about communication	
		reading about Washington, D.C.	Discussing the U.S. Capitol
5	Past Tense of Irregular Verbs	simple past	Improvising dialogue
		present perfect	Talk about travel
		past perfect	Write freely about travel
	Unusual Expresions:	*a couple/give a ring/make it/*etc.	
		practice conversation using unusual expressions	Discuss U.S national makeup
		read and discuss background of Americans	- National Politics

Week	Basic Skill Feature	Skill Practice	Expected Functional Skill Acquistion
6	Modal Auxilia-ries: Ability Necessity Obligation - Advisability Permission Possibility	study meaning added to verb by modal compose sentence with varied meaning and tenses	Write short composition using the various modal auxiliaries
7	Modal Perfects: Advisability Volition Conditional Conditioned - Result Habitual Customary Action	*might/should/ could* *would*	Read and analyze story for deep meaning
8	Inferred Cer-tainty Inferred Prob-ability Possibility Permission Request Prediction Ability	*must/can't* *should* *may/could/can* *can/will/shall* read: *Statue of Liberty*	Write composi-tion on govern-ment based on fact or fiction Talk about the meaning of the Statue of Liberty and other known monuments

Week	Basic Skill Feature	Skill Practice	Expected Functional Skill Acquistion
9	The Conditional Neutral Wish Future	"if" + present past tense present	Tell about things that you wish for
10	Special Expressions	Provided (that) Providing (that) in the event that-whether...or read about the Grand Canyon	Write short composition about plans and things to do, using special expresions Discuss travel and sights
11	The Unreal, Untrue Past Contrary to fact conditions	"if" Clause past perfect tense "so long as" "unless"	Talk about international events Discuss cultural differences
12	Uses of "if"	as *conditional* as *time* as *contrast* as *degree* read *Mardi Gras*	Write short composition about government

Week	Basic Skill Feature	Skill Practice	Expected Functional Skill Acquistion
13	The Passive Voice	practice different tenses practice conversation using the passive voice read about "Indy"	Talk about different customs in the U.S. — compare customs of nationalities Write about sports
14	Direct Statement Direct Quote Reported Speech(Indirect Statement) Quotation Mark Colon Wh - Questions	practice writing dialogue using the structures learned *why/where/what/ when/who/how*	Compare cultural differences Write on a cultural topic
15	Comprehensive Review and Evaluation		Writing freely on subjects requiring vocabulary sophistication Dictating letters on various assigned topics Translating from native language to English on assigned topics Prepared for college English composition

ESL CERTIFICATION EVALUATION UPON COMPLETION OF THE ADVANCED ESL COURSE

Part I   Listening Comprehension

A. The examinee will hear a series of remarks or questions. He/she is to choose the most appropriate response indicated in the answer book.

B. The examinee will hear a dialogue and a news broadcast, provided by a brief background description and followed by four spoken questions. The examinee must choose the answer to each question from choices on answer sheet.

C. The examinee will hear a conversation among several speakers. He/she must listen attentively to the main ideas and general character of spoken material and decide whether each of eight statements following it is true or false.

Part II   Dictation

The candidate will hear five brief sentences. He/she will write exactly what is said, including punctuation. This is a test of a person's ability to recognize sound/letter correspondence in English.

Part III   Reading Comprehension (CLOZE Test)

The examinee will read three passages with blanks spaced every five words. He/she will choose the appropriate word from a choice of three. This is a test of overall control of vocabulary and structures necessary for reading in English.

Part IV   Oral Proficiency Test

The candidate will be interviewed by at least two professors in English. The interview consists of questions designed to elicit specific grammatical structures, vocabulary and pronunciation problems in English.

This is a test of an individual's ability to speak English. The candidate will be graded on his/her fluency, pronunciation, control of grammatical structures and command of vocabulary. The following is a chart and description of the co-occurring factors in speaking proficiency. The examinee will be evaluated on the basis of these factors. (Adapted from the method used at the Foreign Service Institute, U.S. State Department, Washington, D.C.)

The factors identified for evaluation are *accent, comprehension, fluency, grammar*, and *vocabulary*. Numerical value is assigned to each factor to suit a particular need and situation.

A sample Oral Proficiency Test is included on the *Let's Continue* CD/Tape recording.

CHECK-LIST TO DETERMINE RATINGS*

Weighting Table							
	1	2	3	4	5	6	(A)
Accent	0	1	2	2	3	4	—
Grammar	6	12	18	24	30	36	—
Vocabulary	4	8	12	16	20	24	—
Fluency	2	4	6	8	10	12	—
Comprehension	4	8	12	15	19	23	—

Procedure: Place in column (A) of the table the credits to be given for each scale on the Check-List. For example, a check mark in position 3 on the "Accent" scale is given a credit of 2. Add the credits to find the final score. The final S-rating is to be equated with the total score by the *Conversion Table.*

Conversion Table					
Score	Rating	Score	Rating	Score	Rating
16-25	S-0+	43-52	S-2	73-82	S-3+
26-32	S-1	53-62	S-2+	83-92	S-4
33-42	S-1+	63-72	S-3	93-99	S-4+

*Adopted from similar chart used at the Foreign Service Institute, U.S. State Department, Washington, D.C.

END-OF-TRAINING CHECK LIST - EVALUATION UNIT

Name _____   Date _____
Agency _____   Time _____
Social Sec. No. _____   Linguist _____
Date Of Birth _____   Language _____

1. **Accent**   foreign   ___:___ ___:___ ___:___ native
2. **Grammar**   inaccurate ___:___ ___:___ ___:___ accurate
3. **Vocabulary**   inadequate ___:___ ___:___ ___:___ adequate
4. **Fluency**   uneven   ___:___ ___:___ ___:___ even
5. **Comprehension** incomplete___:___ ___:___ ___:___ complete

Absolute Rating: S-_____

Linguist _____

Instructor _____

Language Proficiency Report

NAME		For Office Use Only
AGENCY	GRADE OF RANK	
SOCIAL SEC. NO.	DATE OF BIRTH	LINGUIST
LANGUAGE	LANGUAGE CODE	
TEST DATE	TESTING PLACE	TEST SCHEDULE
TEST RESULT S-		

REMARKS

RATED BY	REVIEWED BY

ABSOLUTE RATING

"S" SPEAKING PROFICIENCY

S-0 NO PRACTICAL PROFICIENCY

No practical speaking proficiency.

S-1 ELEMENTARY PROFICIENCY

Able to satisfy routine travel needs and
minimum courtesy requirements.

S-2 LIMITED WORKING PROFICIENCY

Able to satisfy routine social demands and limited office requirements.

S-3 MINIMUM PROFESSIONAL PROFICIENCY

Able to speak the language with sufficient structural accuracy and
vocabulary to satisfy representation requirements and handle
professional discussions within a special field.

S-4 FULL PROFESSIONAL PROFICIENCY

Able to use the language fluently and accurately on all
levels perinent to foreign service needs.